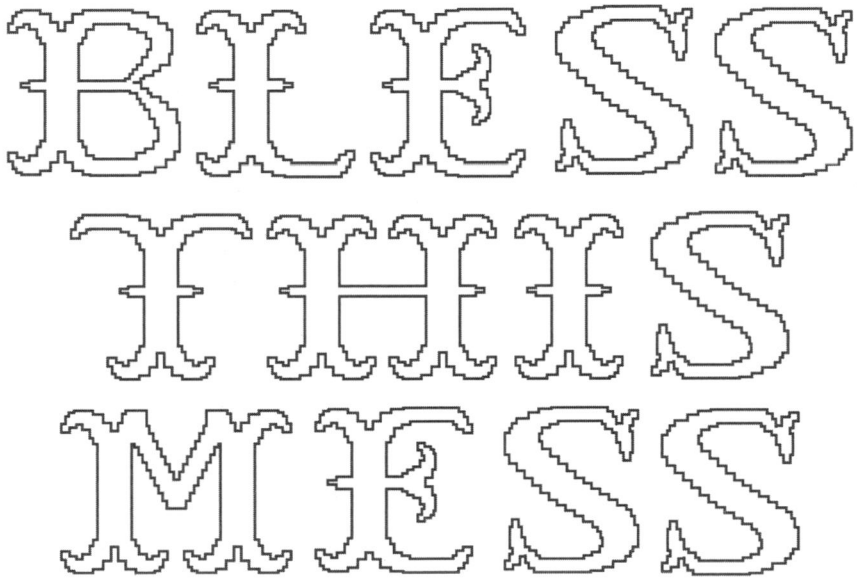


T0120145

# BLESS THIS MESS

## AN EDGY EXPERIENCE FOR THE IRREVERENT COLORIST

JESSICA MAZURKIEWICZ

Racehorse Publishing

Copyright © 2017 by Jessica Mazurkiewicz

All rights reserved. No part of this book may be reproduced in any manner without the express written consent of the publisher, except in the case of brief excerpts in critical reviews or articles. All inquiries should be addressed to Racehorse Publishing, 307 West 36th Street, 11th Floor, New York, NY 10018.

Racehorse Publishing books may be purchased in bulk at special discounts for sales promotion, corporate gifts, fund-raising, or educational purposes. Special editions can also be created to specifications. For details, contact the Special Sales Department, Skyhorse Publishing, 307 West 36th Street, 11th Floor, New York, NY 10018 or info@skyhorsepublishing.com.

Racehorse Publishing™ is a pending trademark of Skyhorse Publishing, Inc.®, a Delaware corporation.

Visit our website at www.skyhorsepublishing.com.

10 9 8 7 6 5 4 3 2 1

Cover design, cover illustration, and interior artwork by Jessica Mazurkiewicz

Print ISBN: 978-1-944686-97-0

Printed in the United States of America

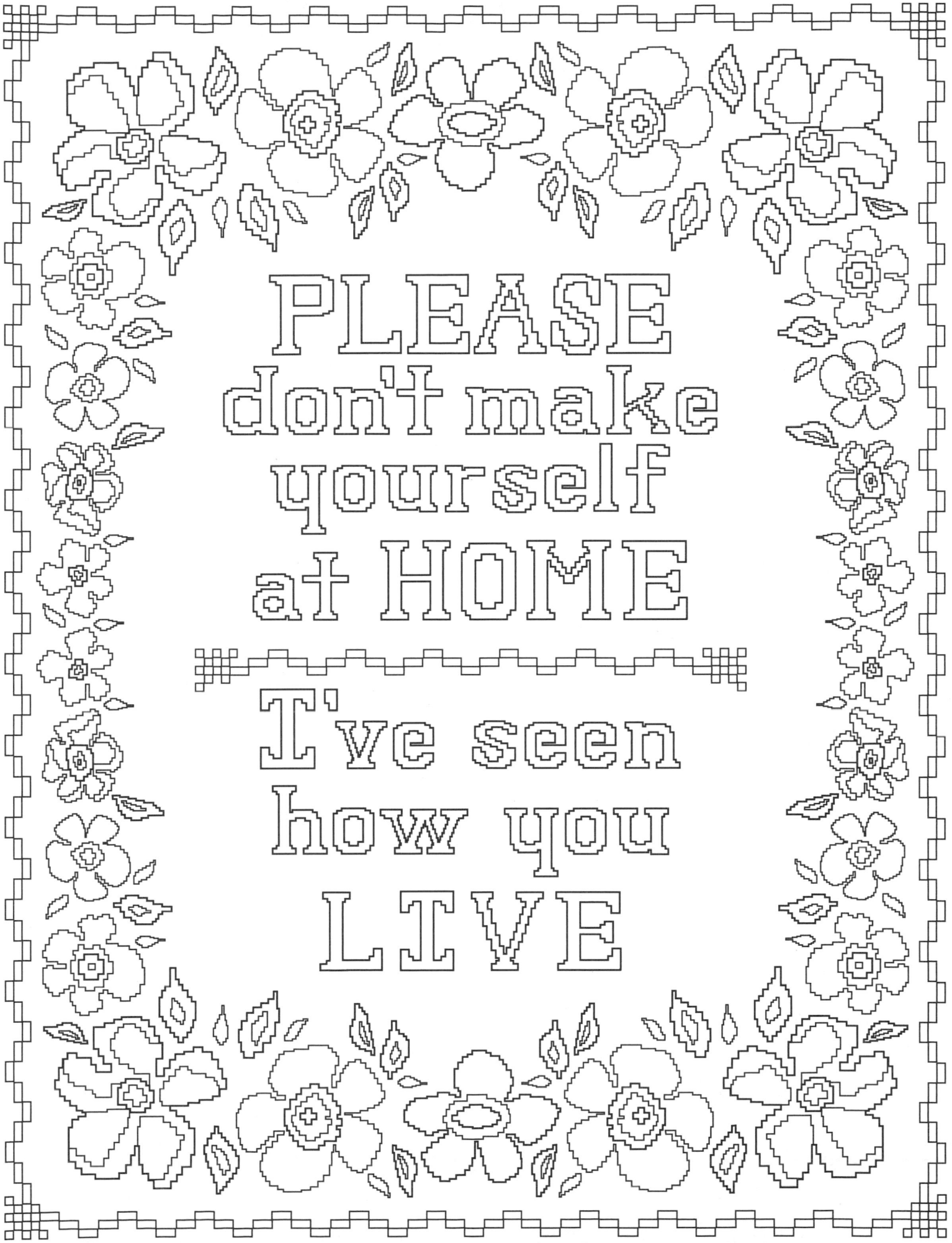
PLEASE
don't make
yourself
at HOME
I've seen
how you
LIVE

← 1

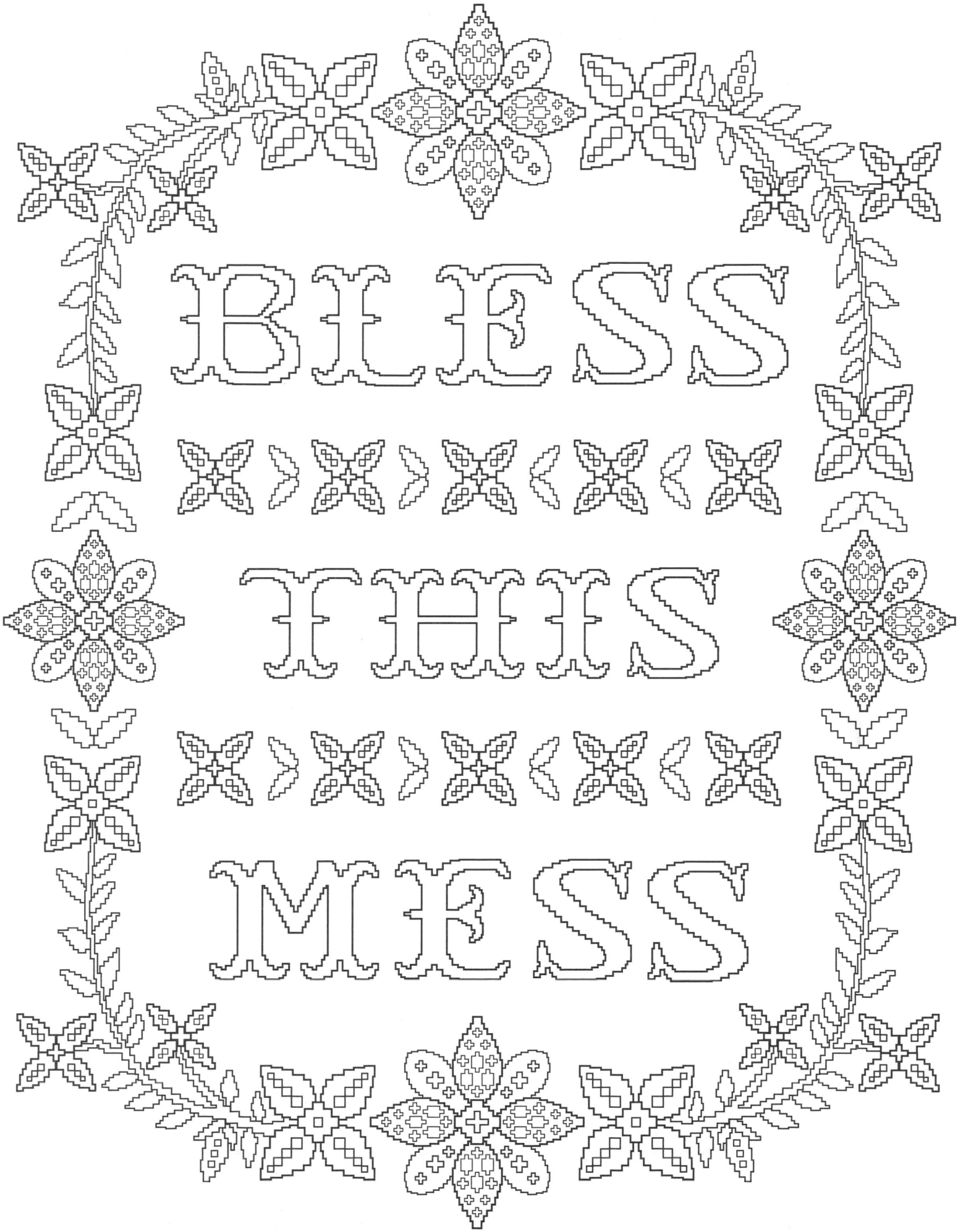
BLESS
THIS
MESS

← 2

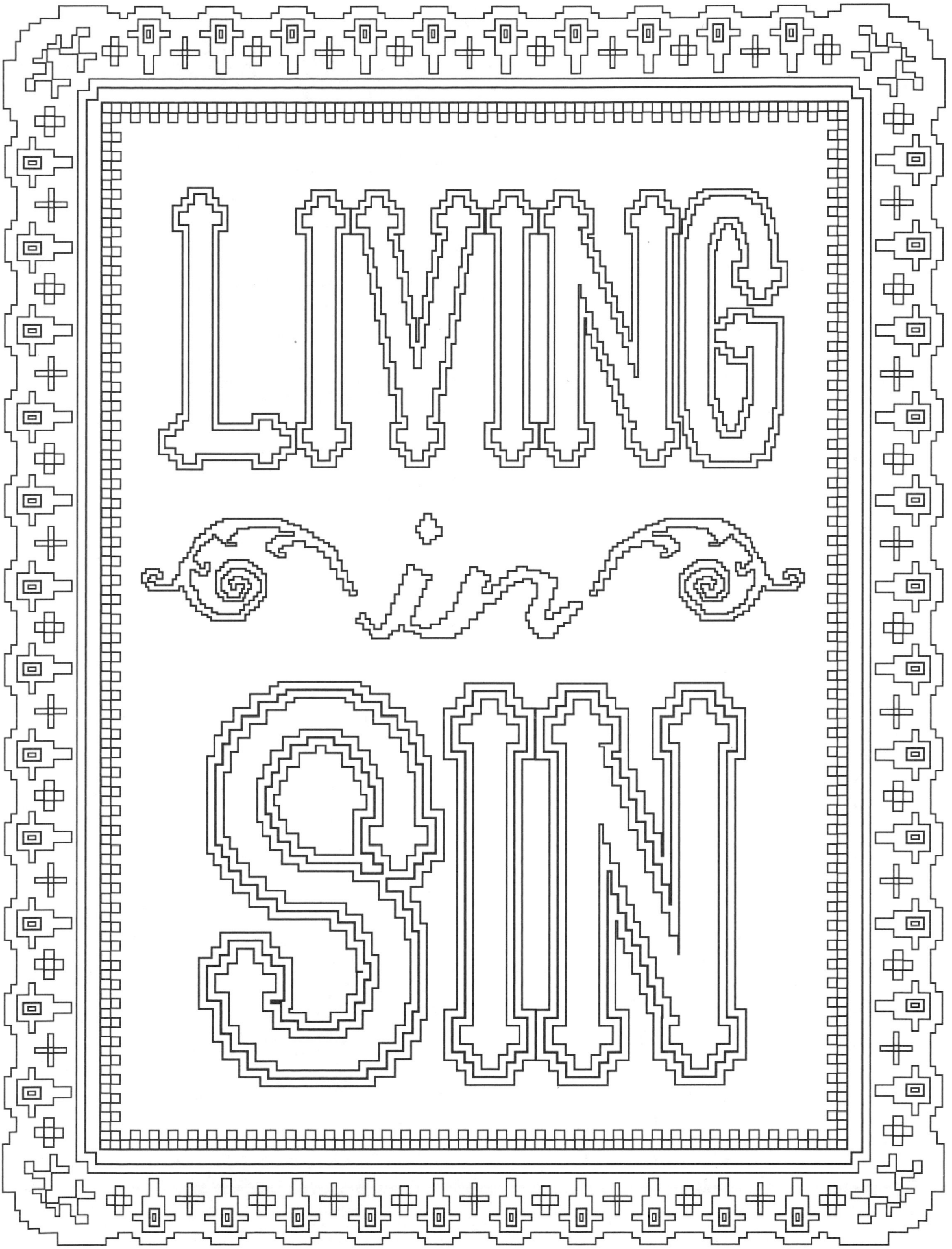
LIVING
in
SIN

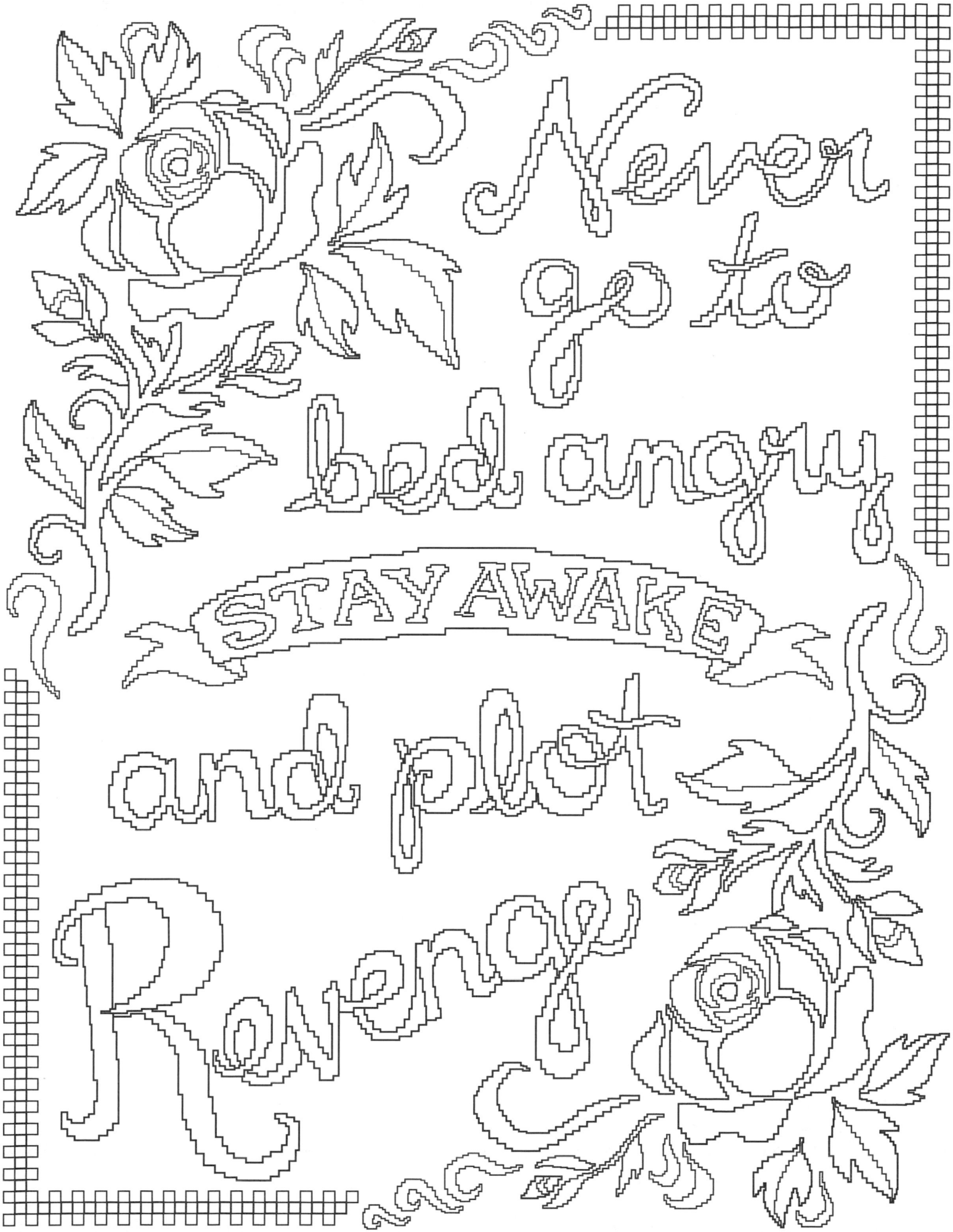
Never go to bed angry
STAY AWAKE
and plot
Revenge

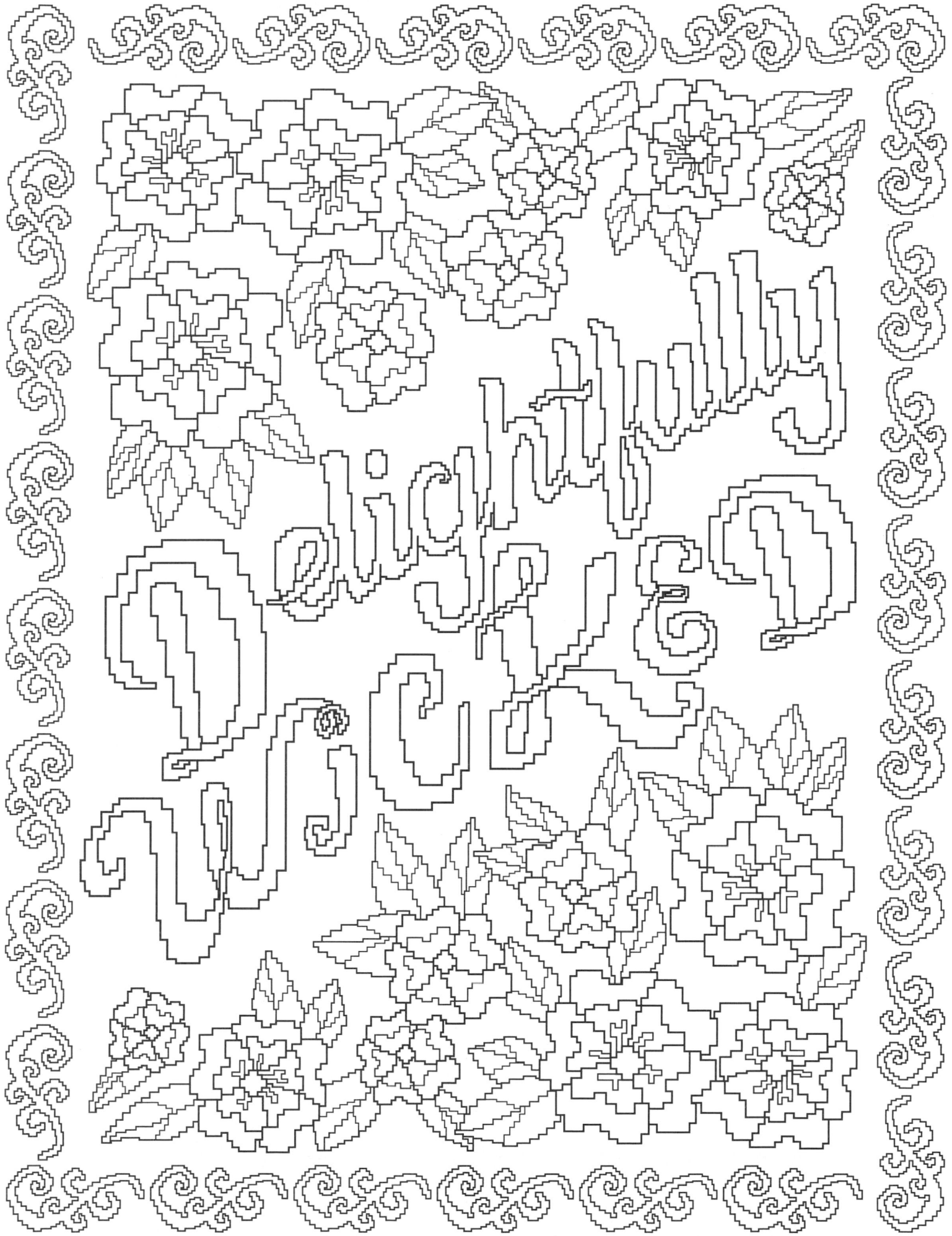
Beautiful
Recipes
Nice

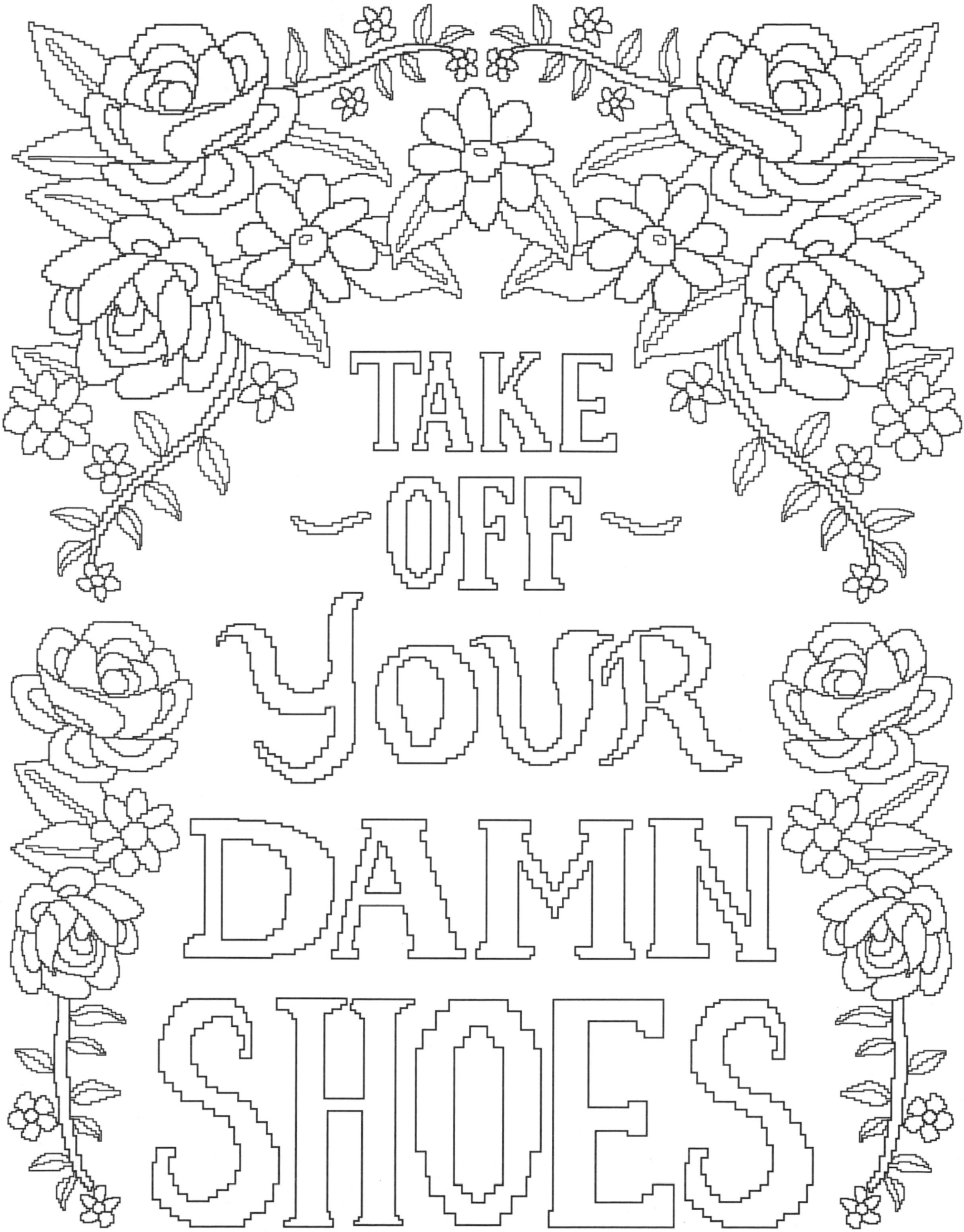
TAKE
OFF
YOUR
DAMN
SHOES

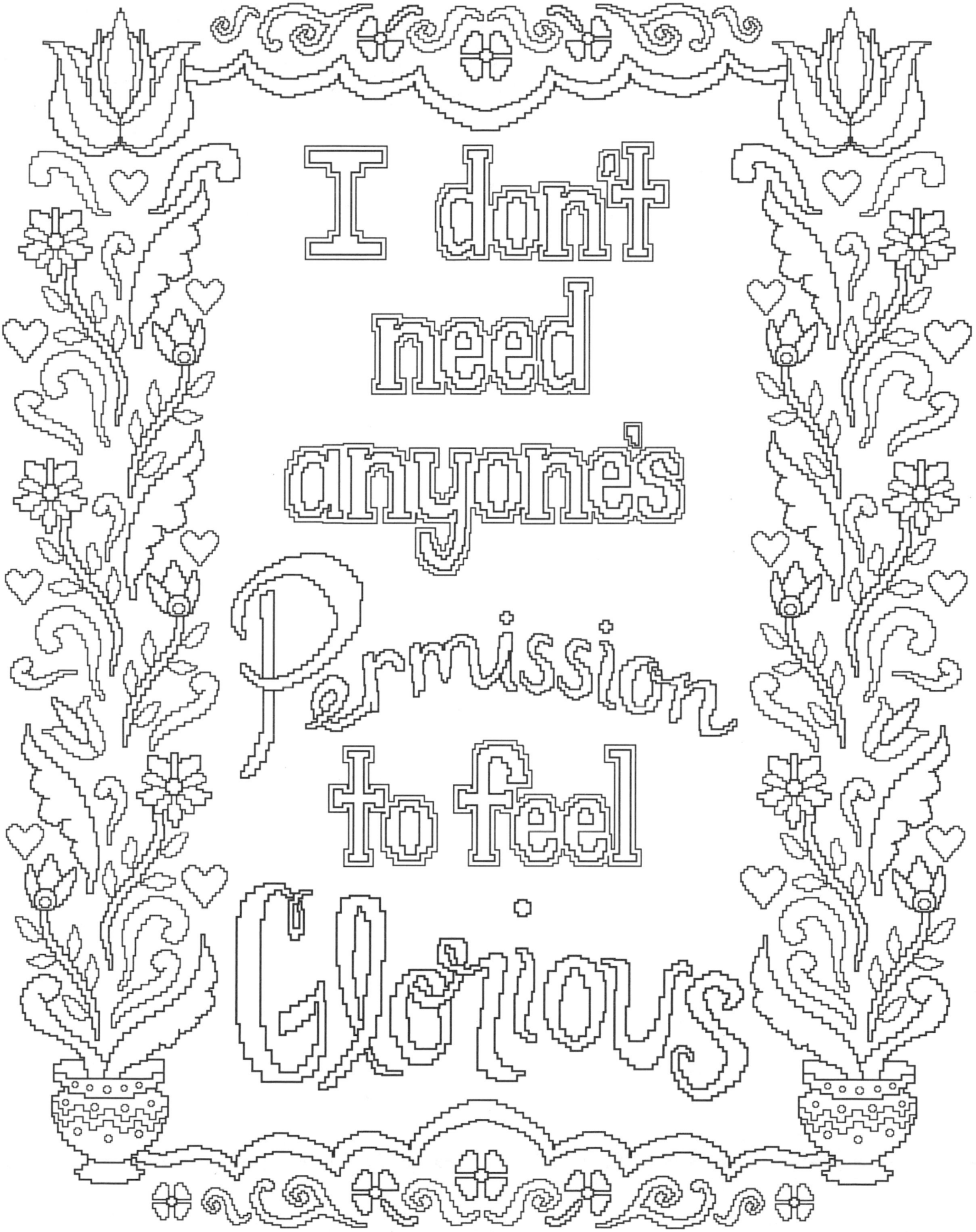
I don't
need
anyone's
permission
to feel
Glorious

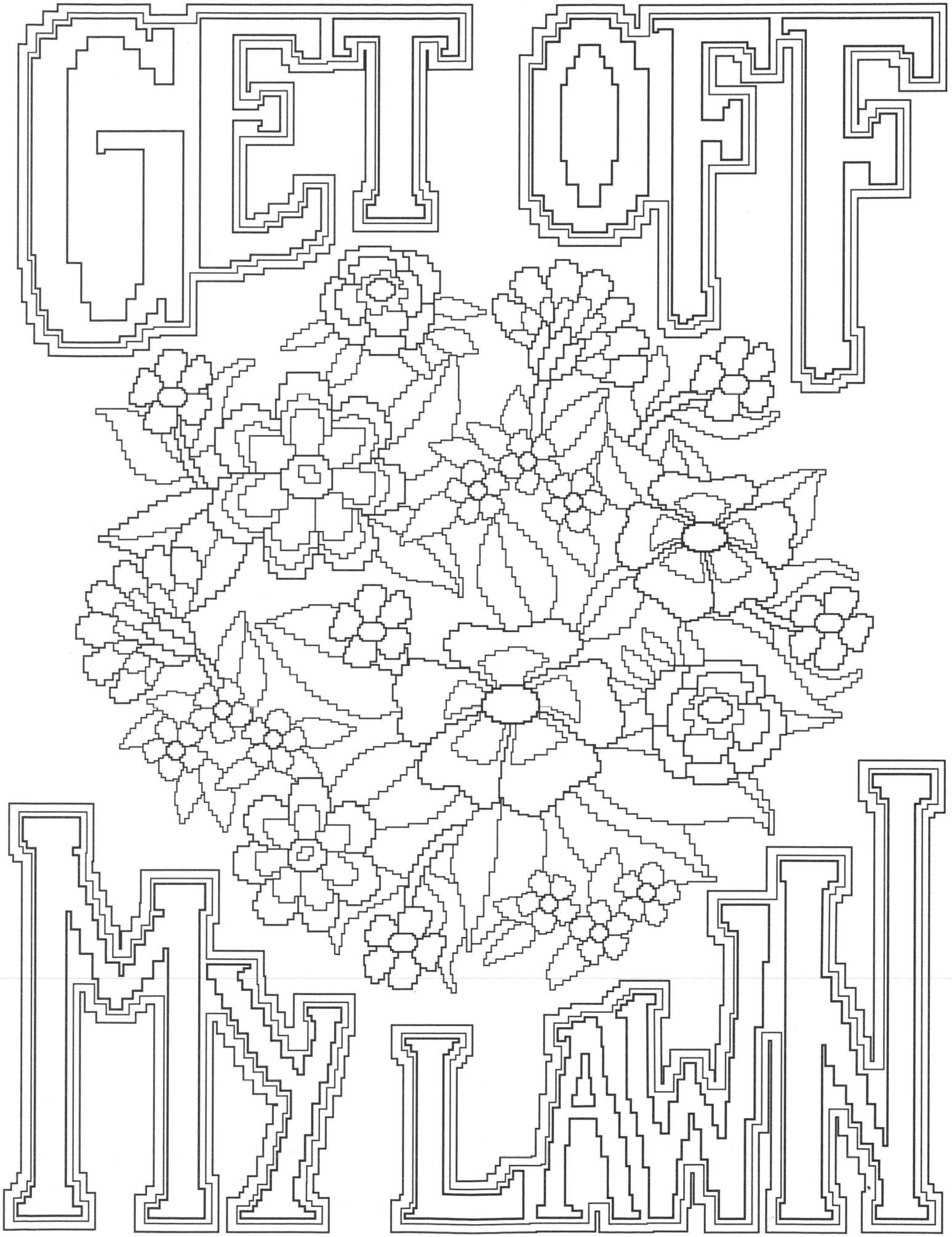
GET OFF
MY LAWN

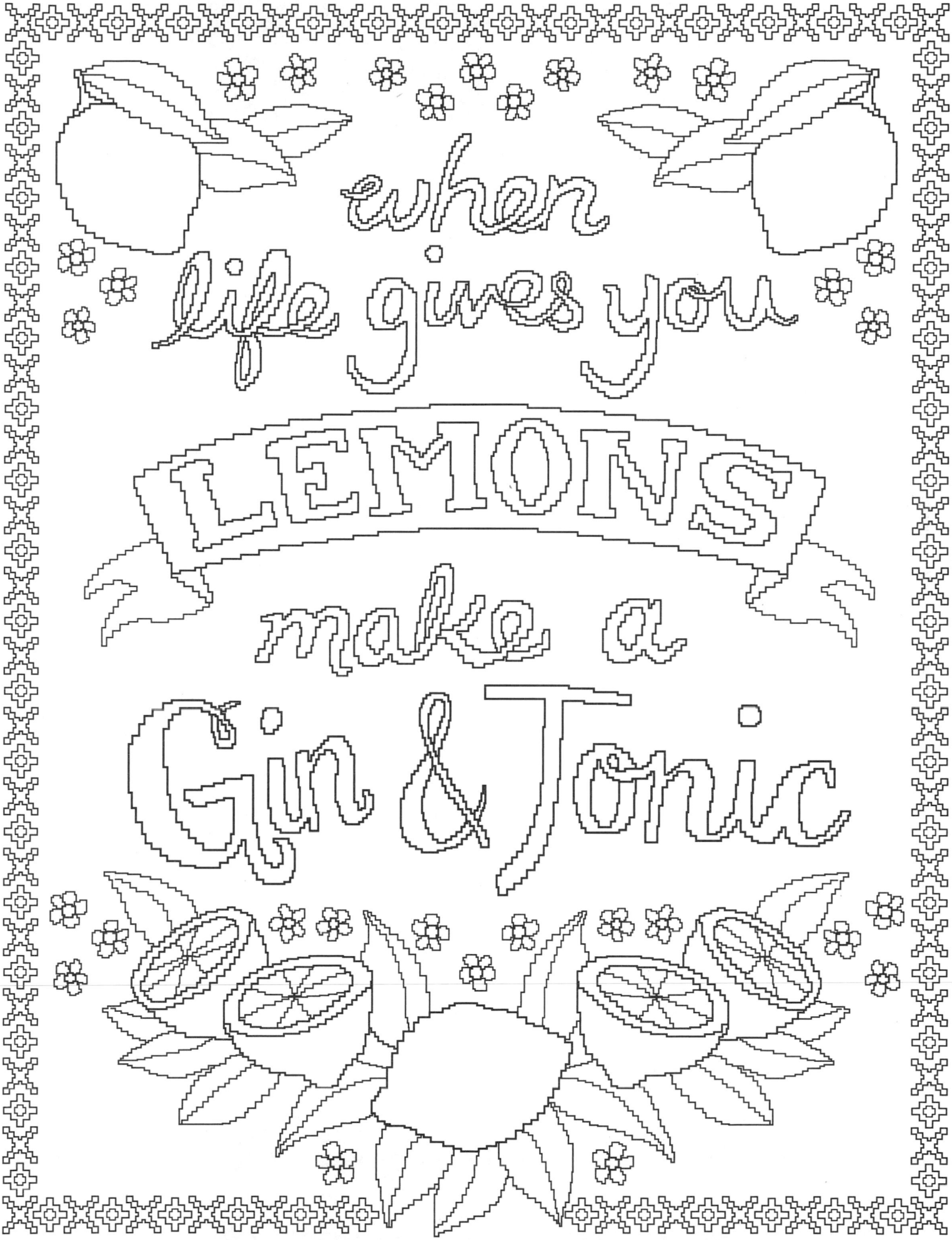
when
life gives you
LEMONS
make a
Gin & Tonic

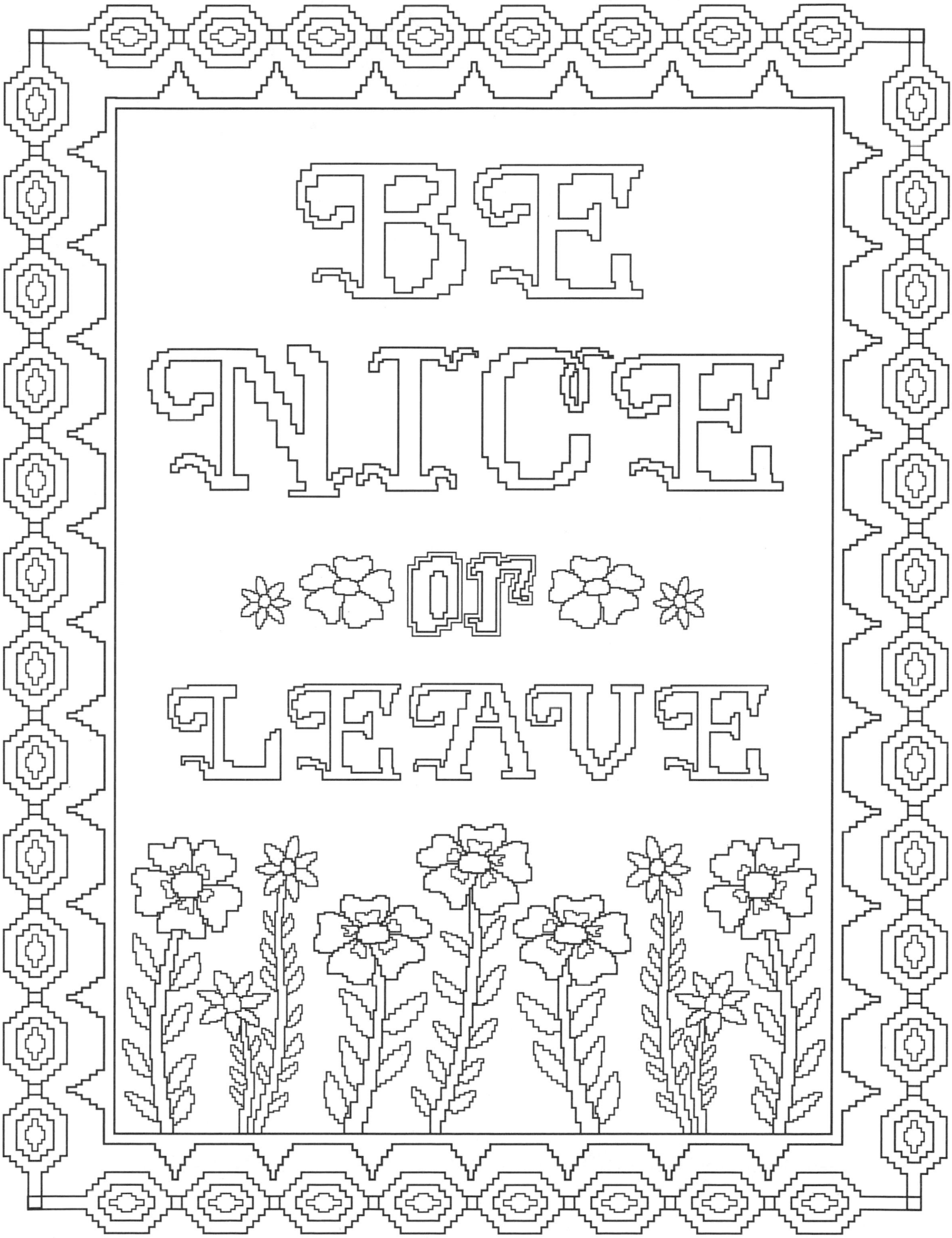
BE
ALICE
OF
LEAGUE

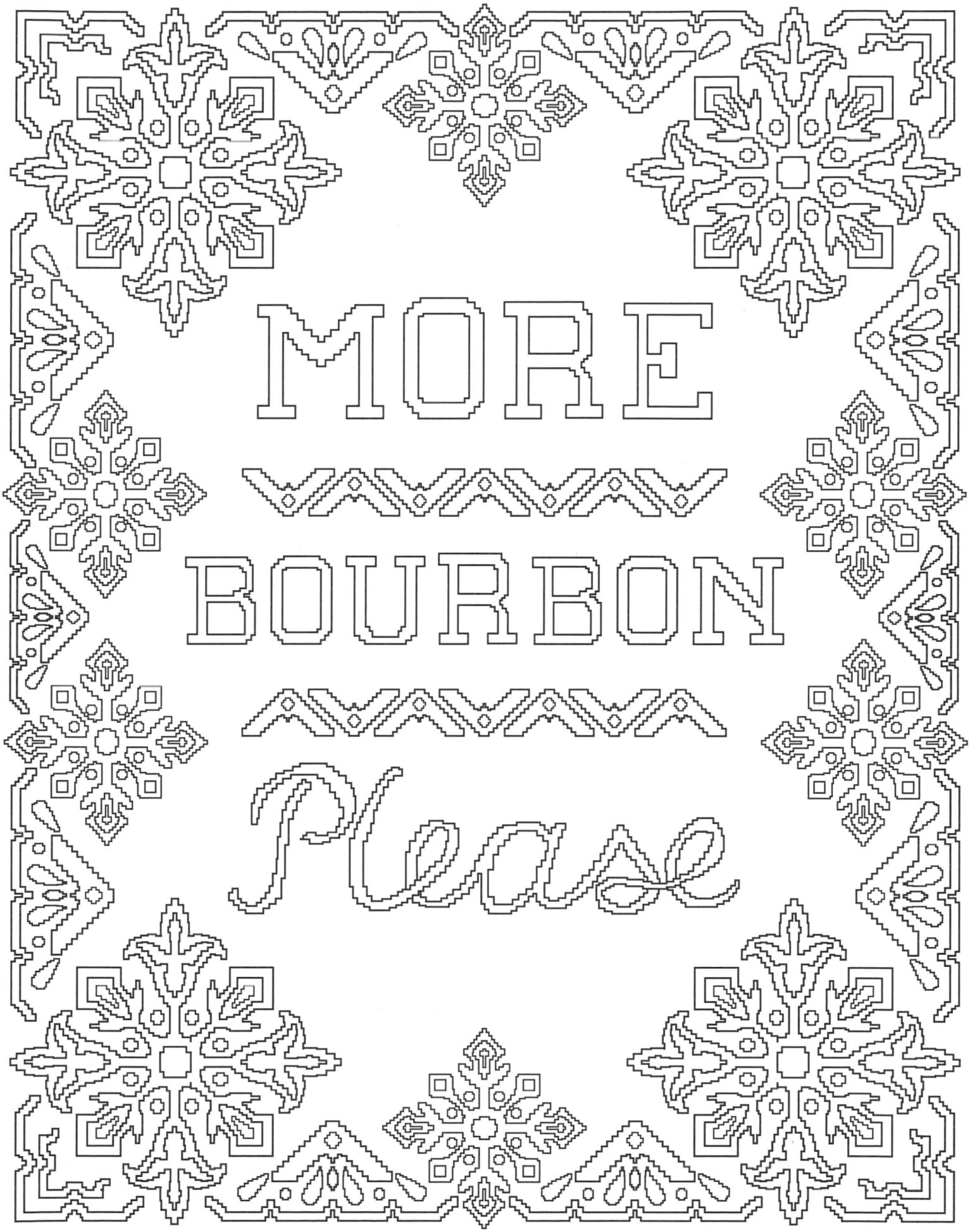
MORE
BOURBON
Please

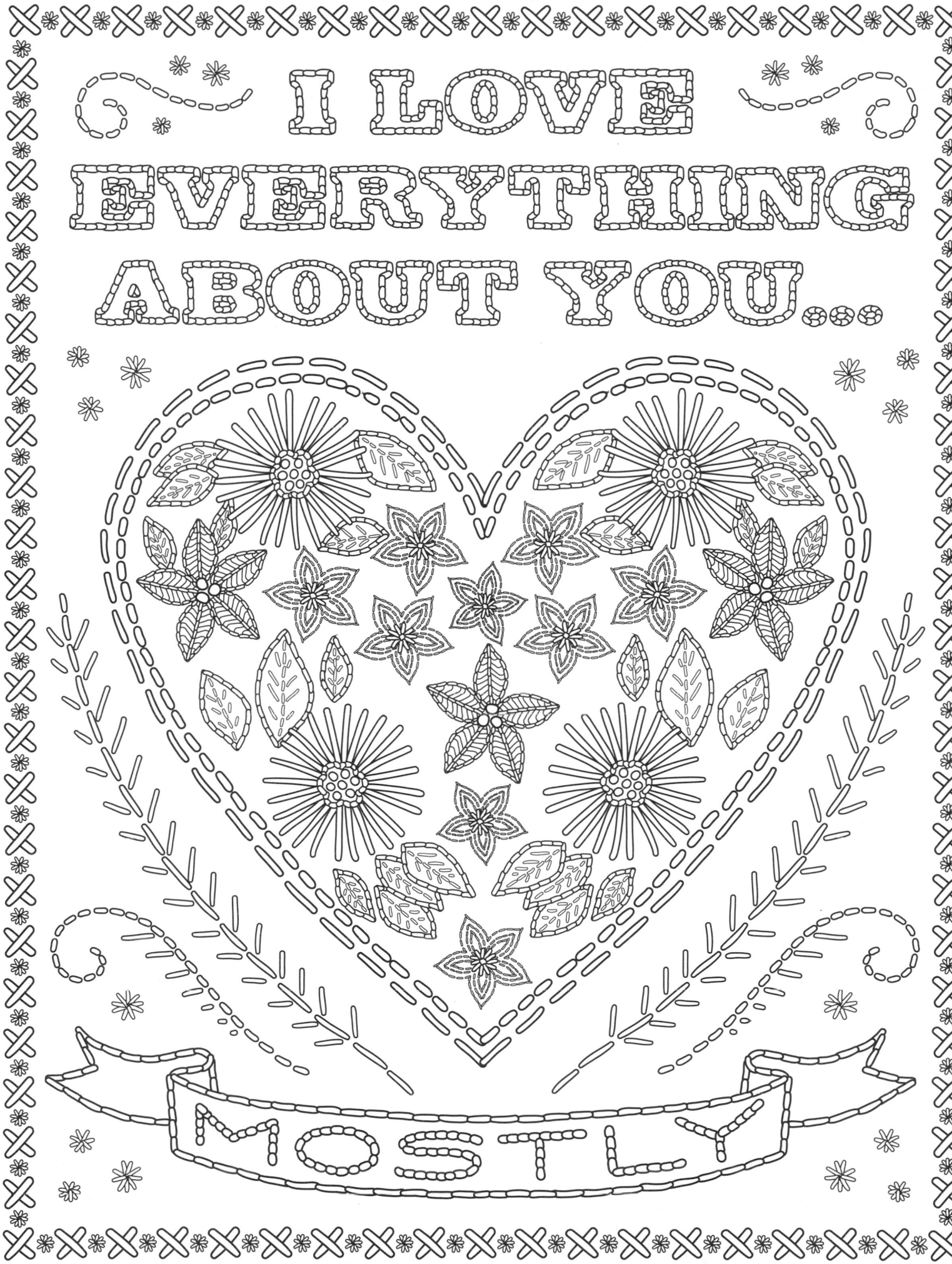
I LOVE
EVERYTHING
ABOUT YOU...
MOSTLY

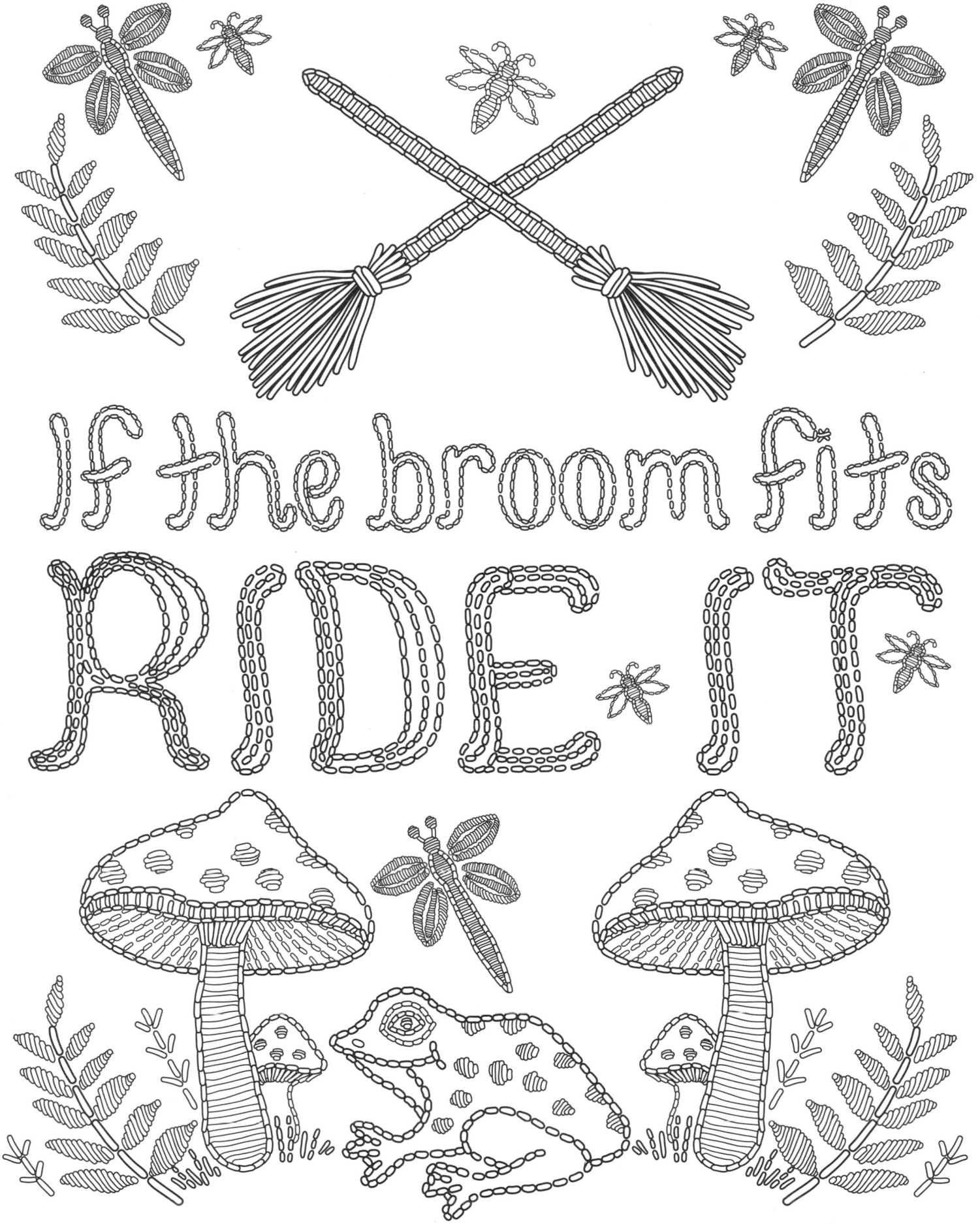
If the broom fits
RIDE IT

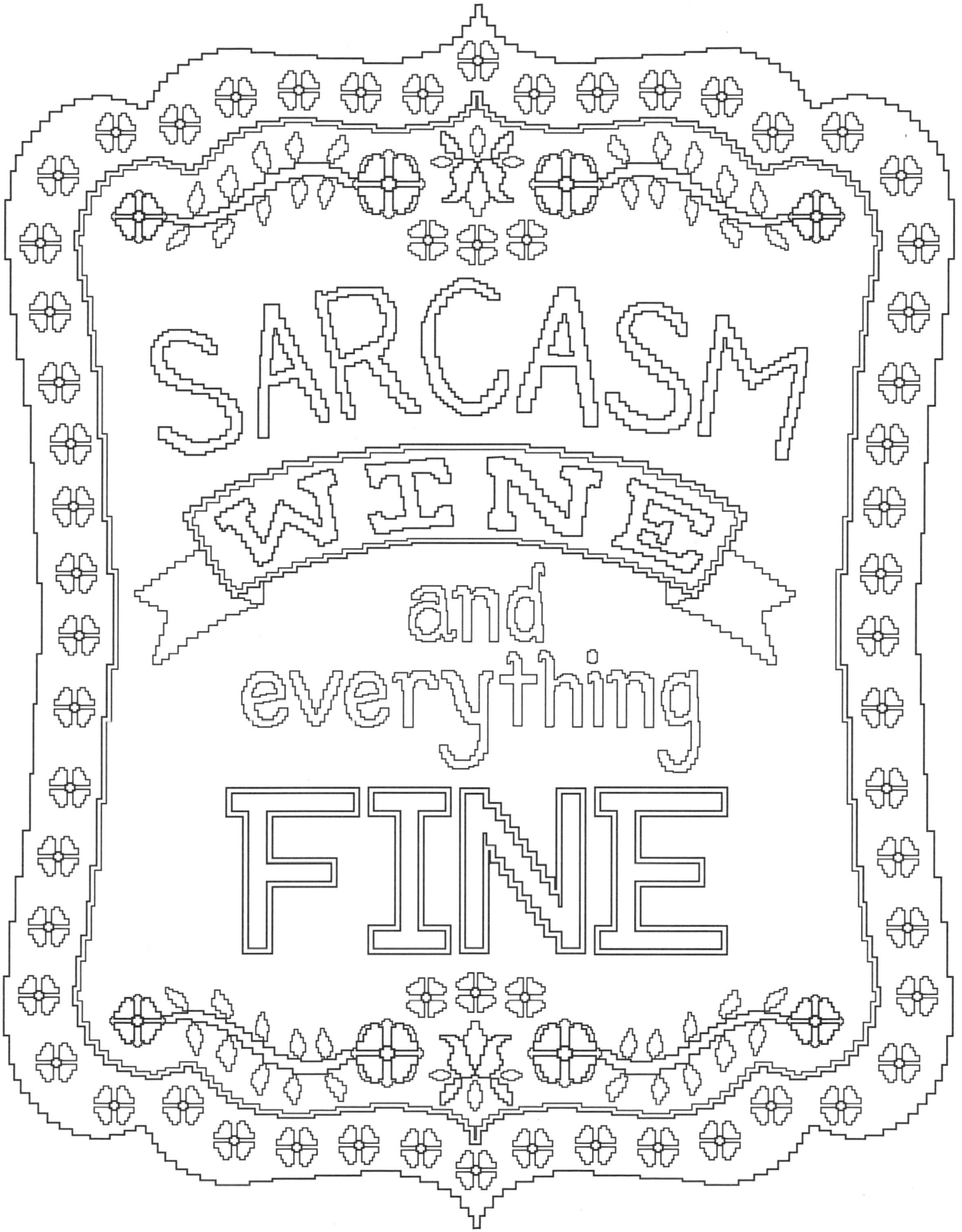
SARCASM
WEINER
and
everything
FINE

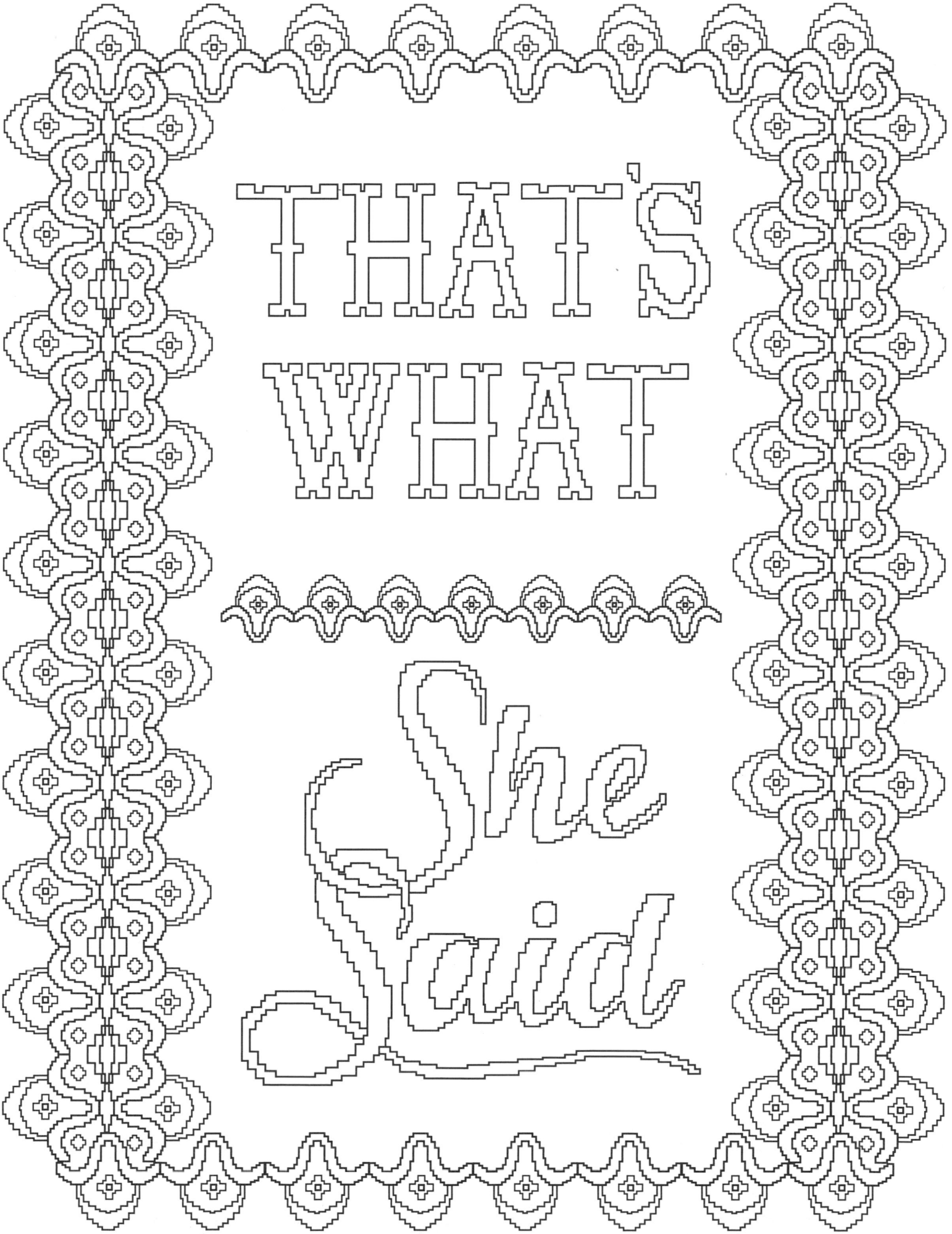
THAT'S
WHAT
She
said

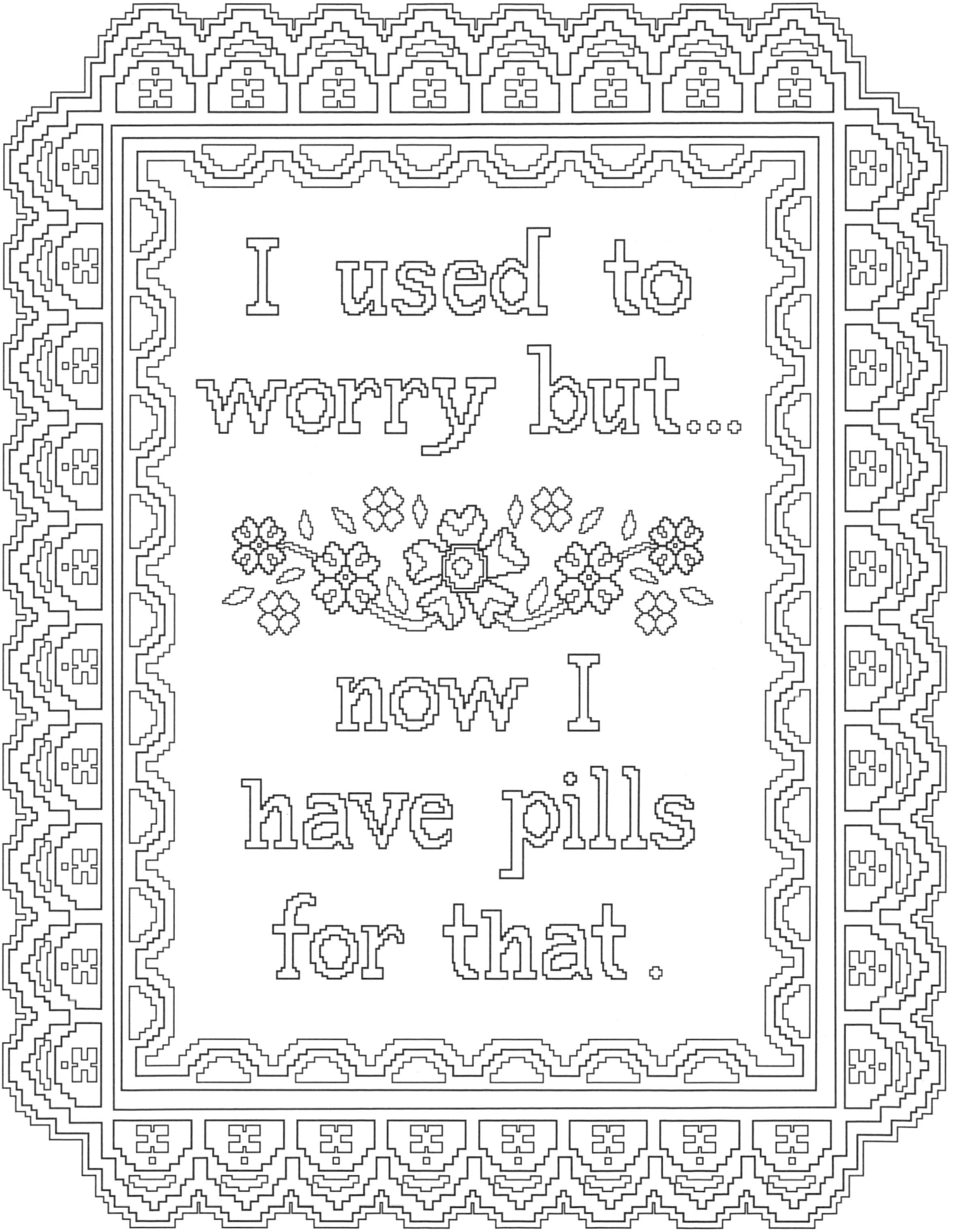
I used to
worry but...
now I
have pills
for that.

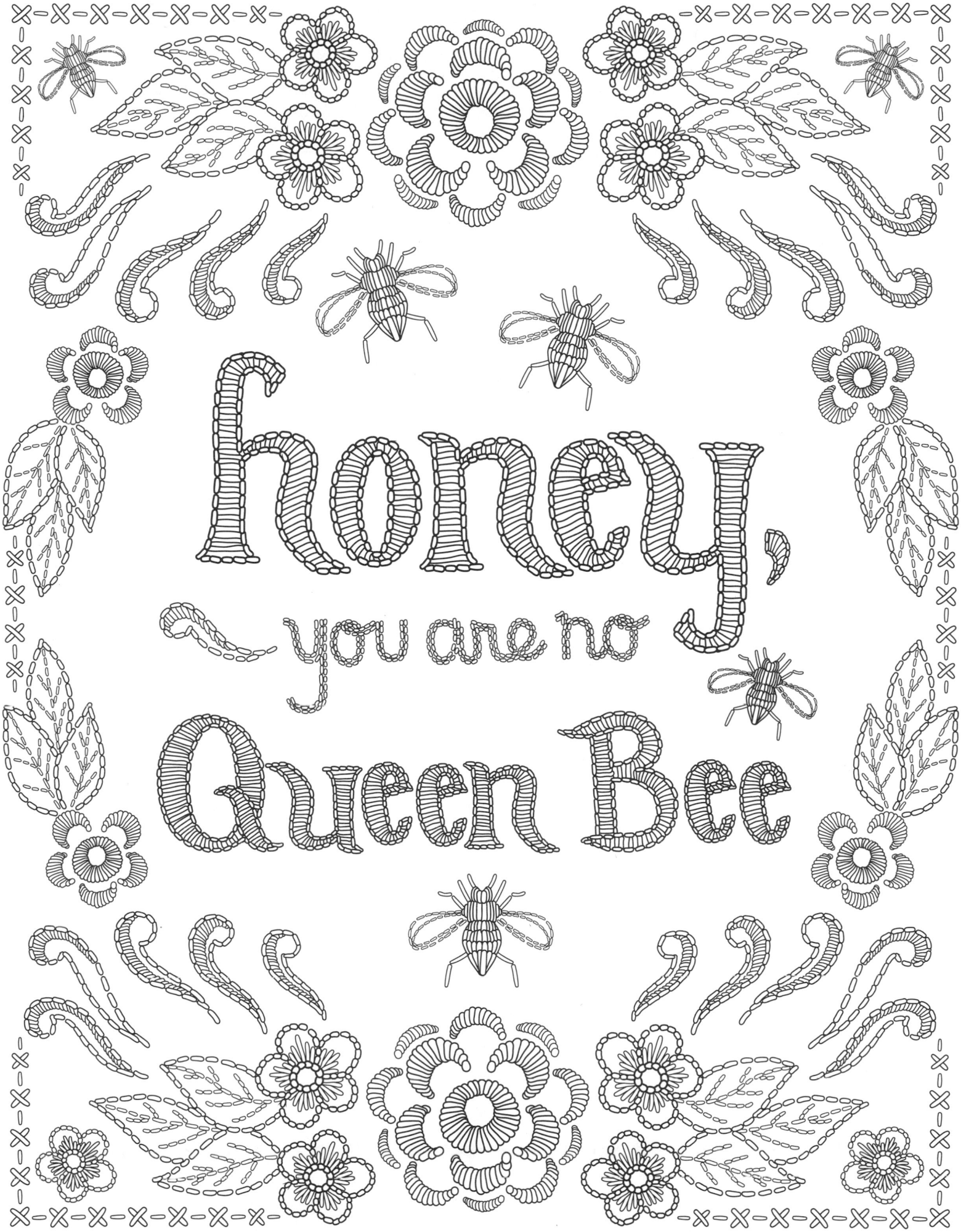
honey,
you are no
Queen Bee

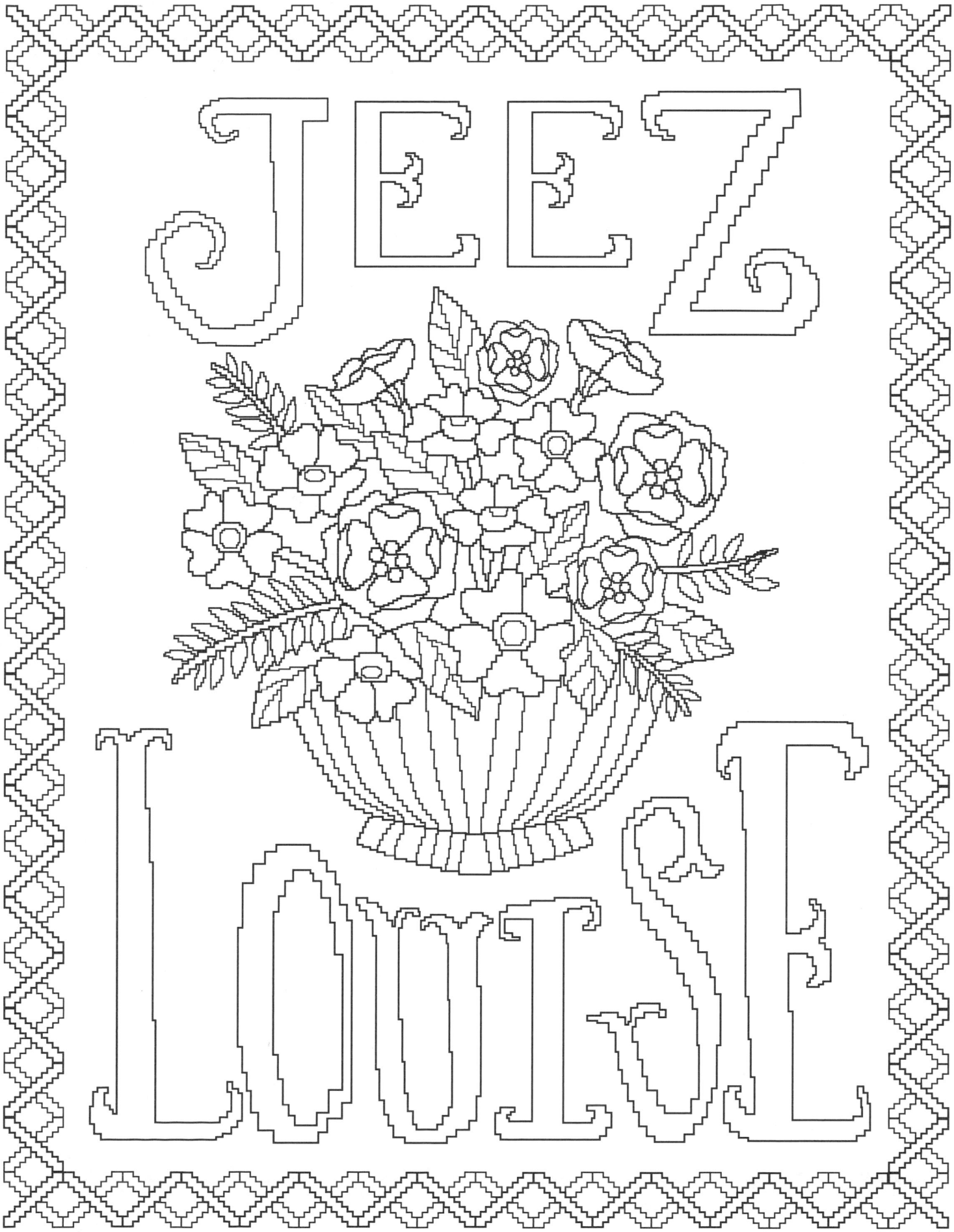
JEEZ
LOUISE

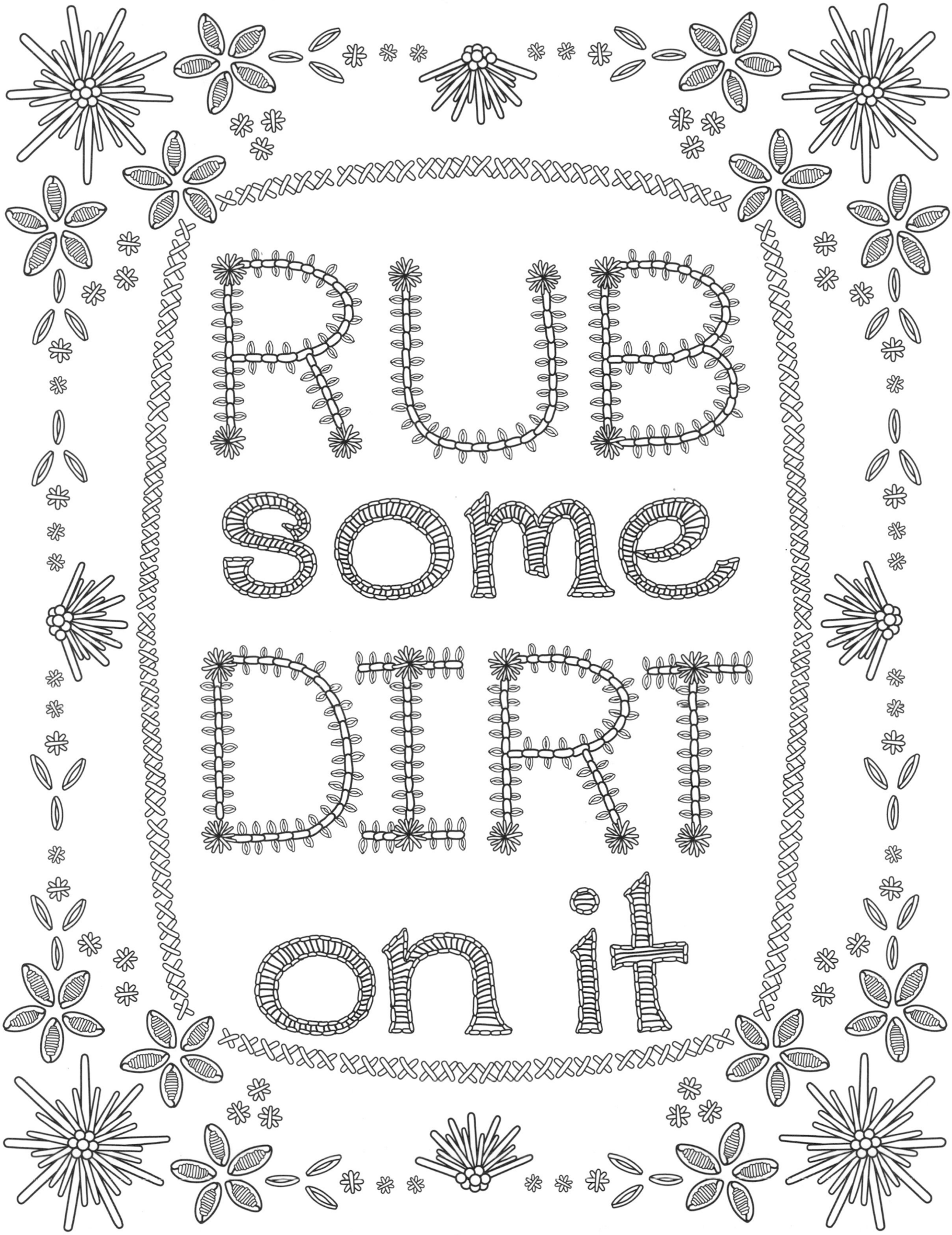
RUB
some
DIRT
on it

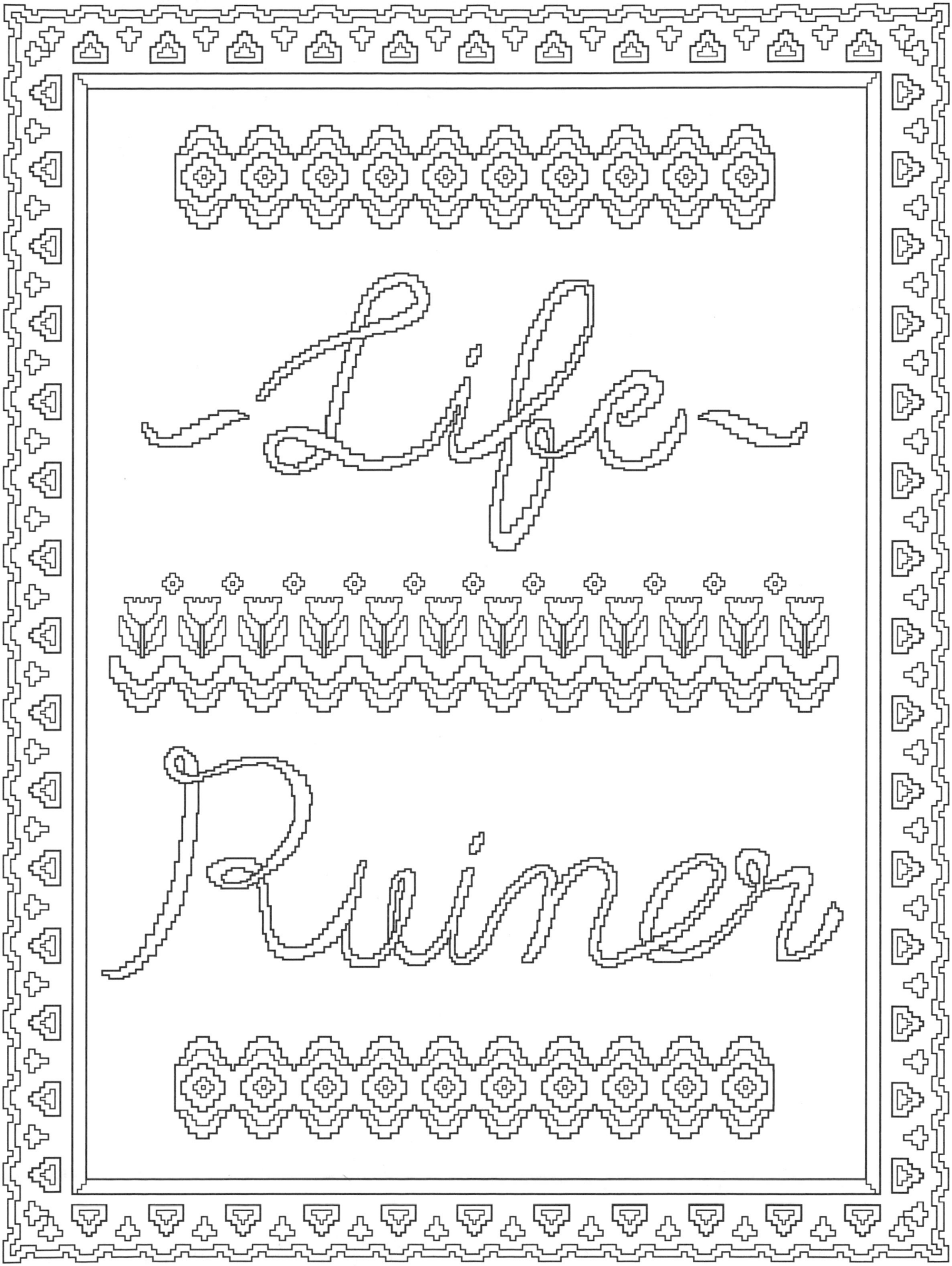
Life
Ruiner

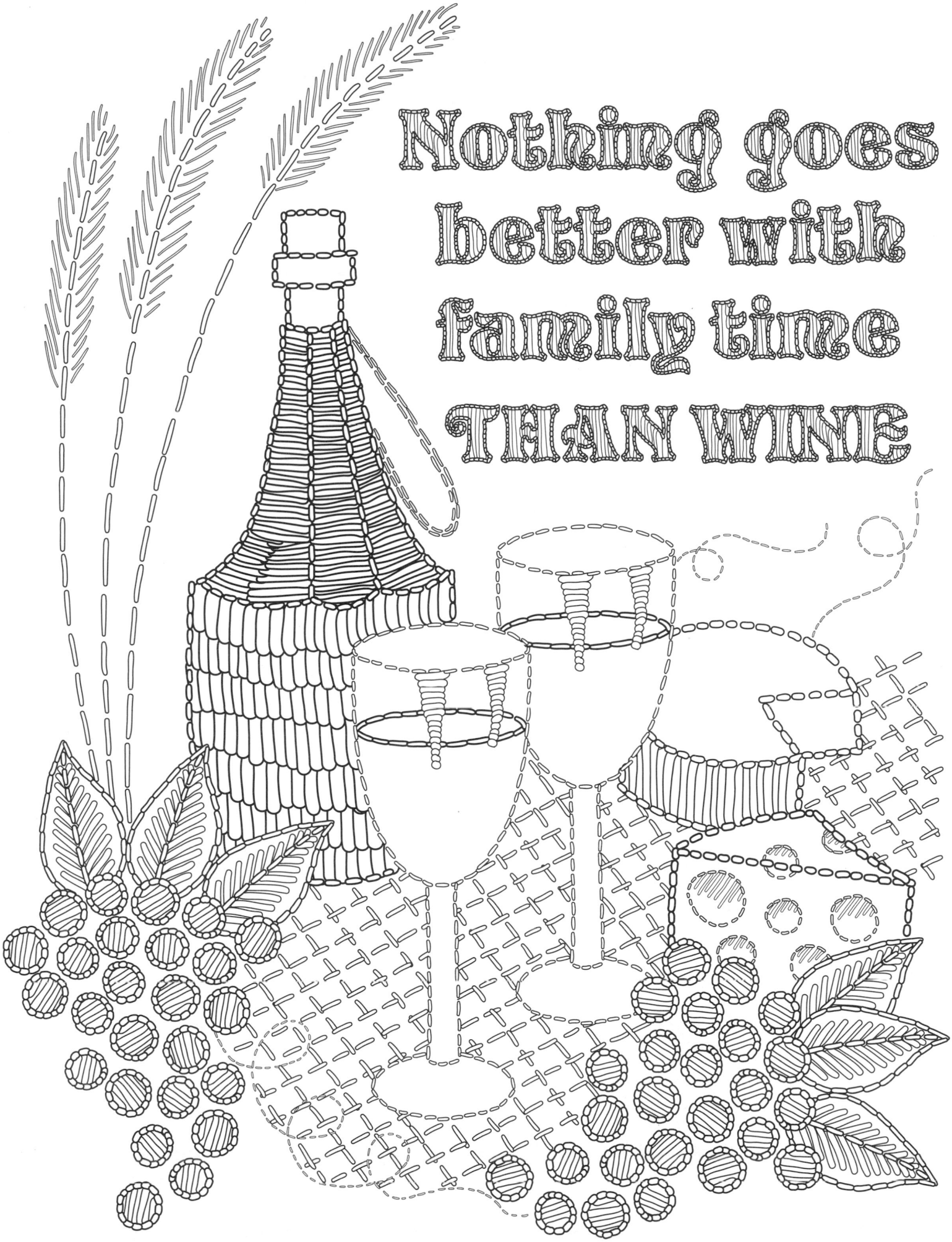
Nothing goes
better with
family time
THAN WINE

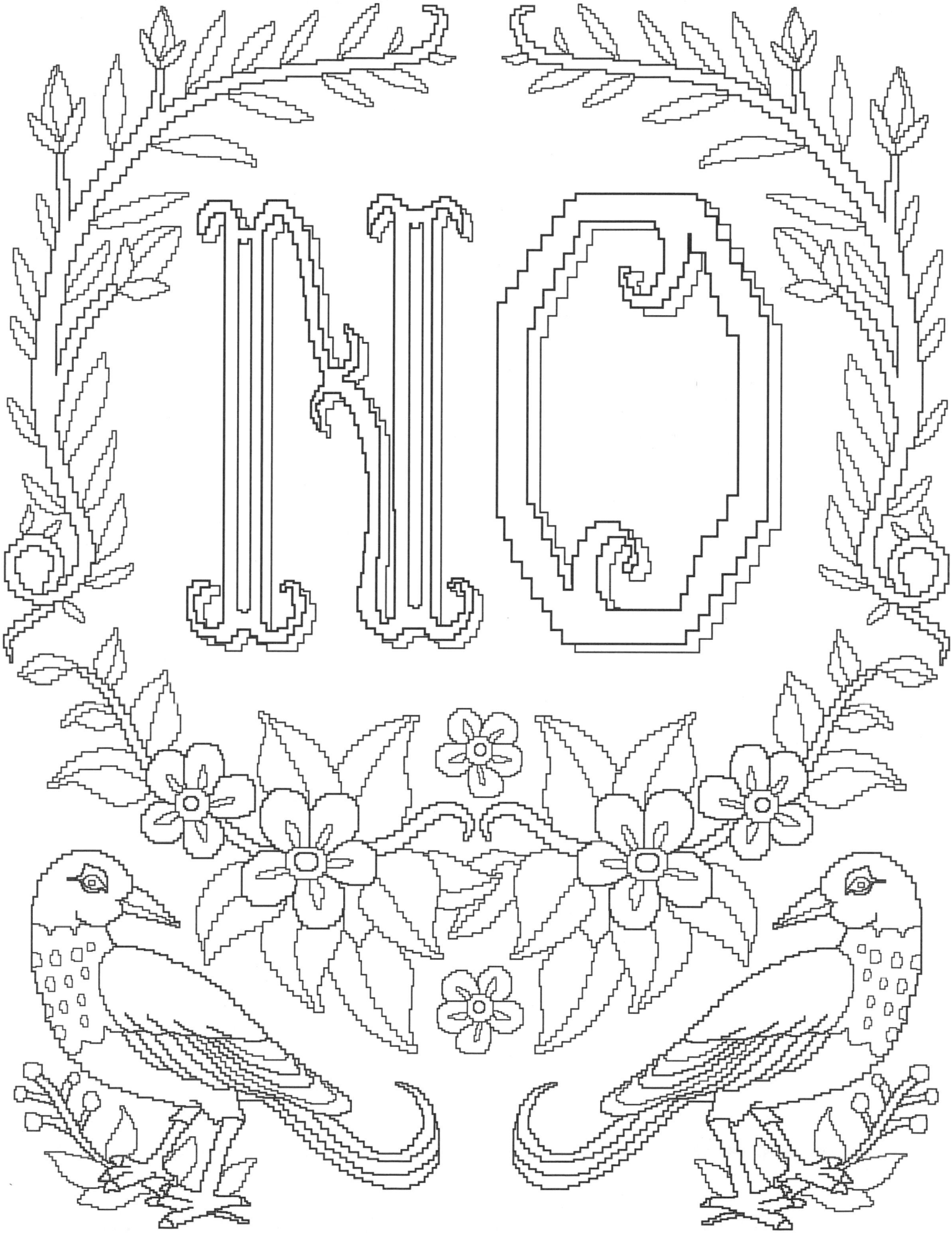

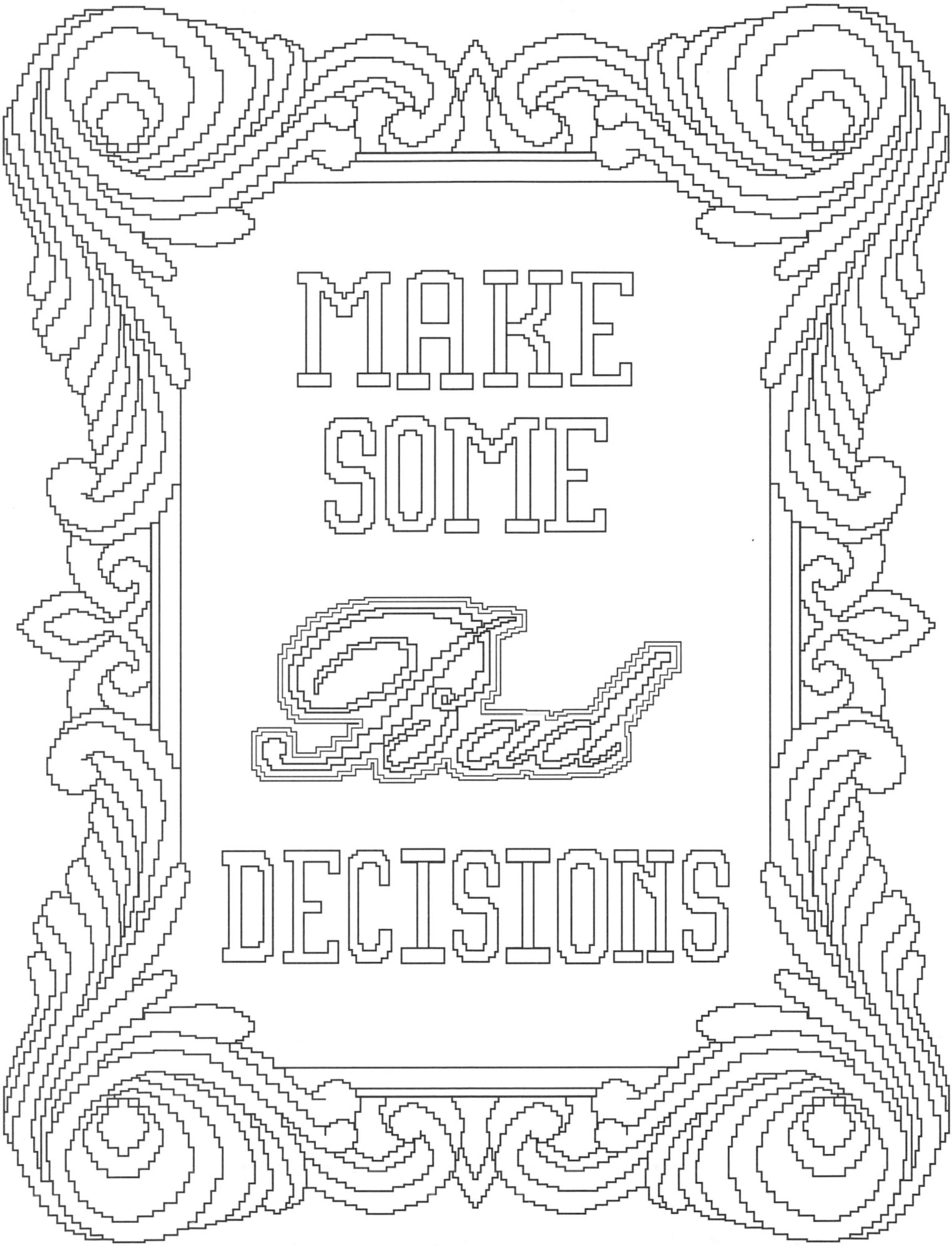
MAKE
SOME
DECISIONS

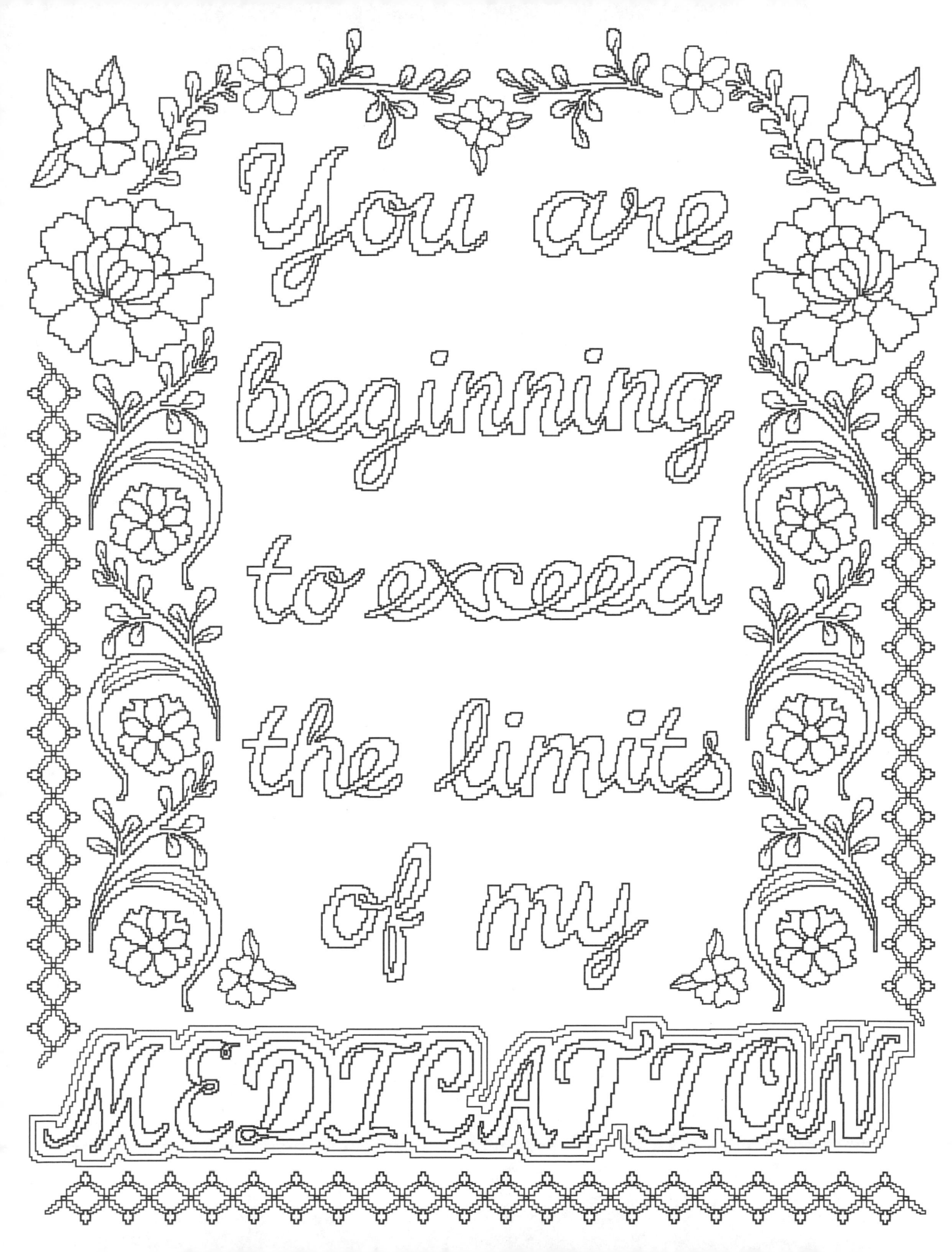
You are
beginning
to exceed
the limits
of my
MEDITATION

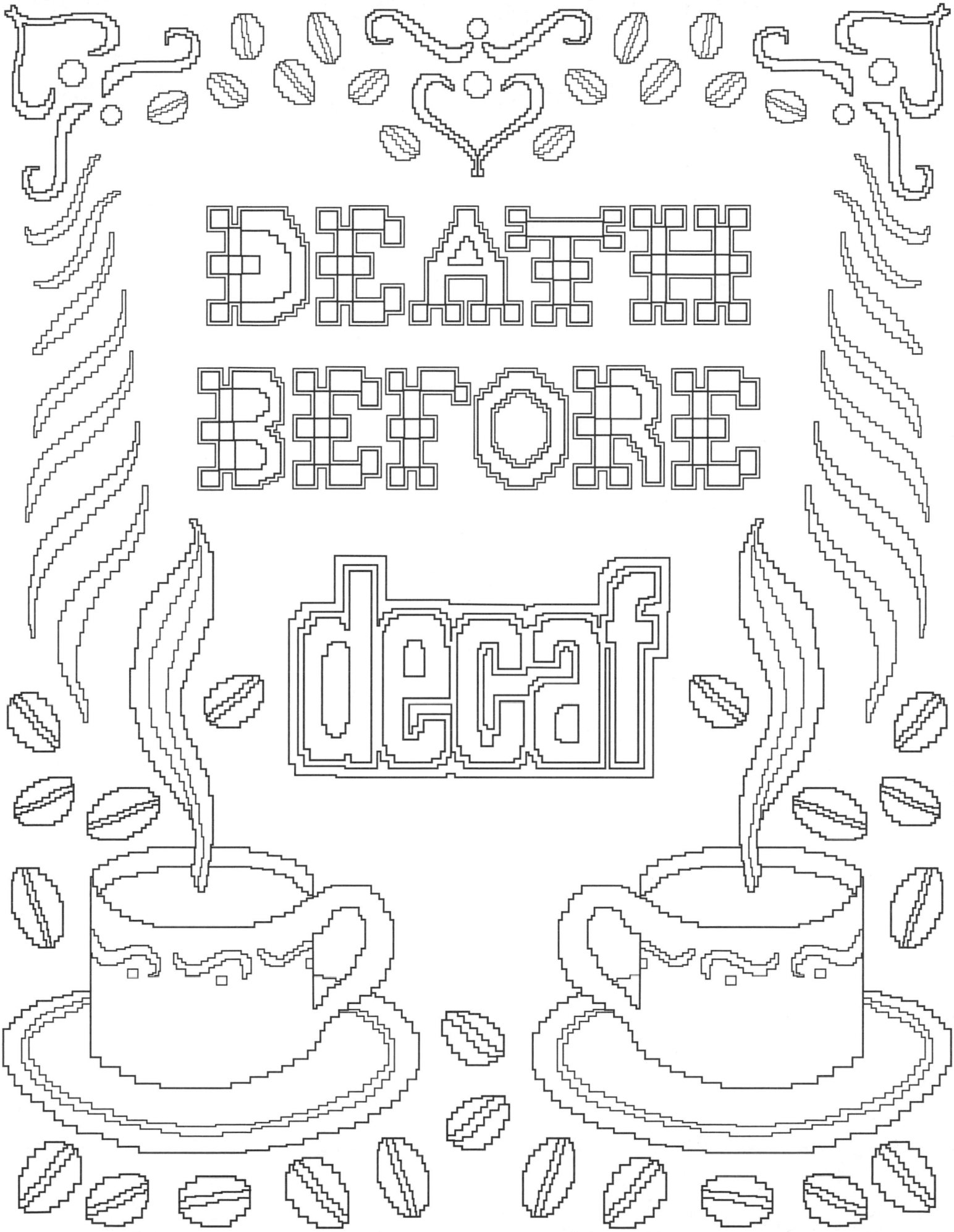
DEATH
BEFORE
decaf

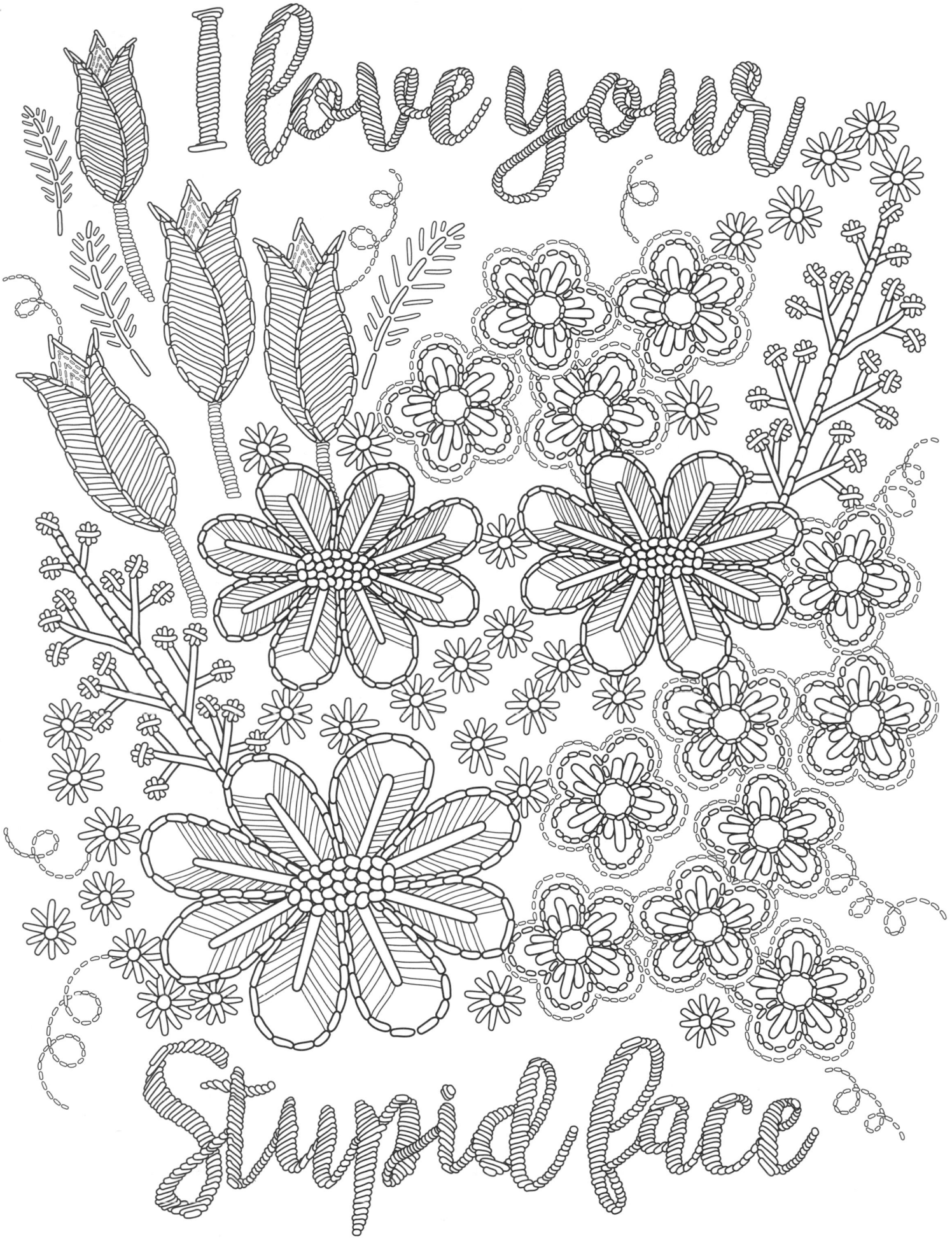
I love your
Stupid face

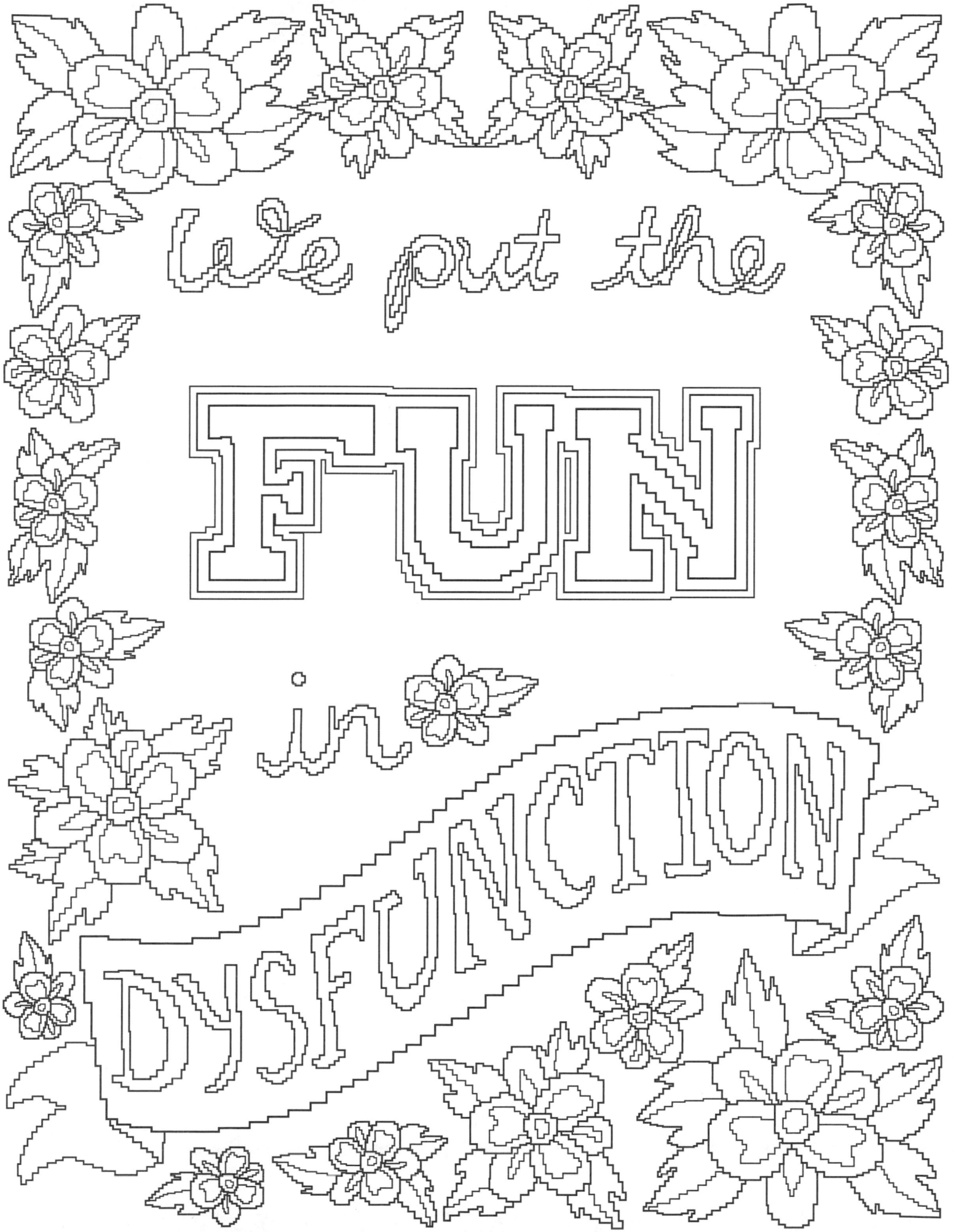
We put the
FUN
in
DISFUNCTION

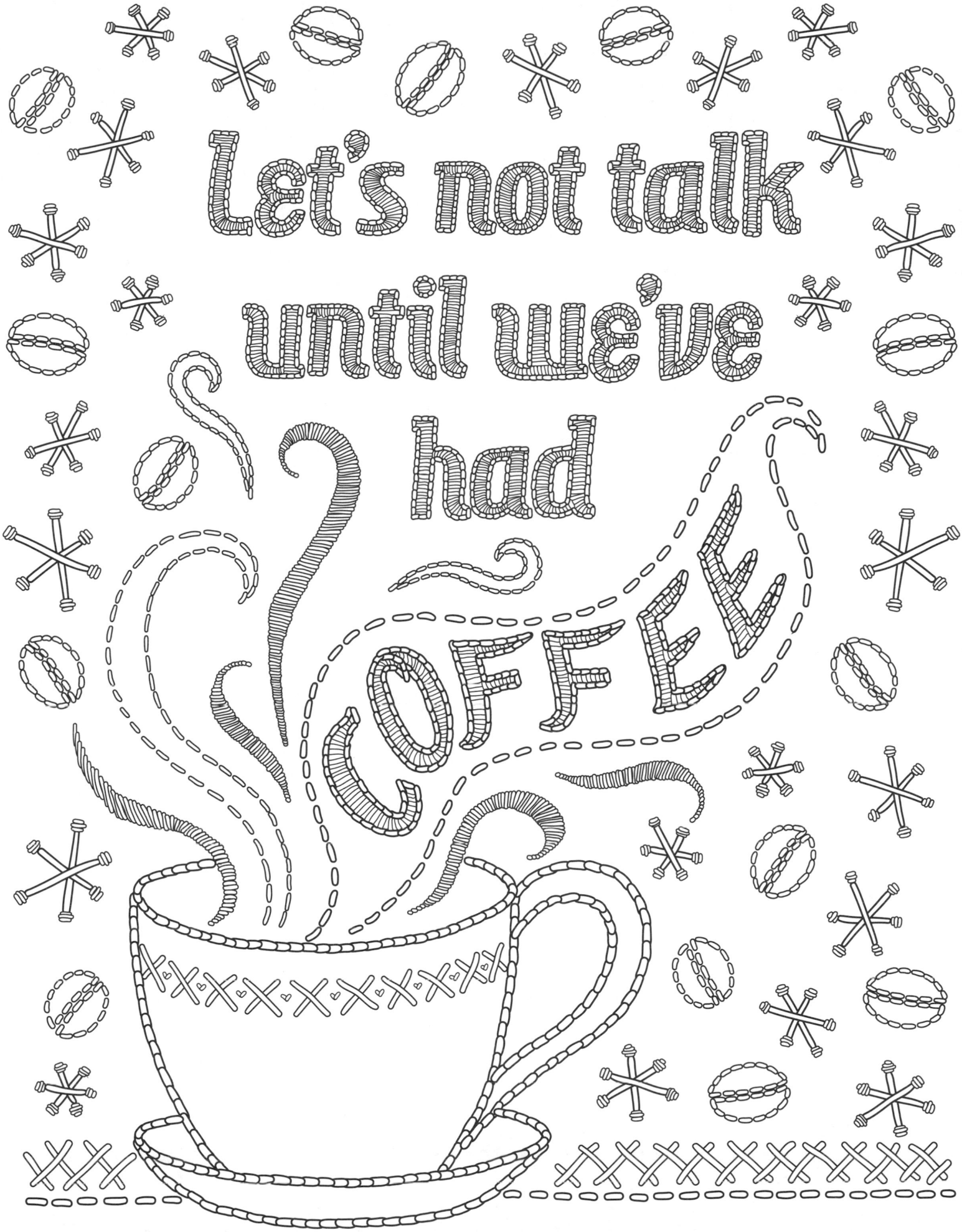
Let's not talk
until we've
had
COFFEE

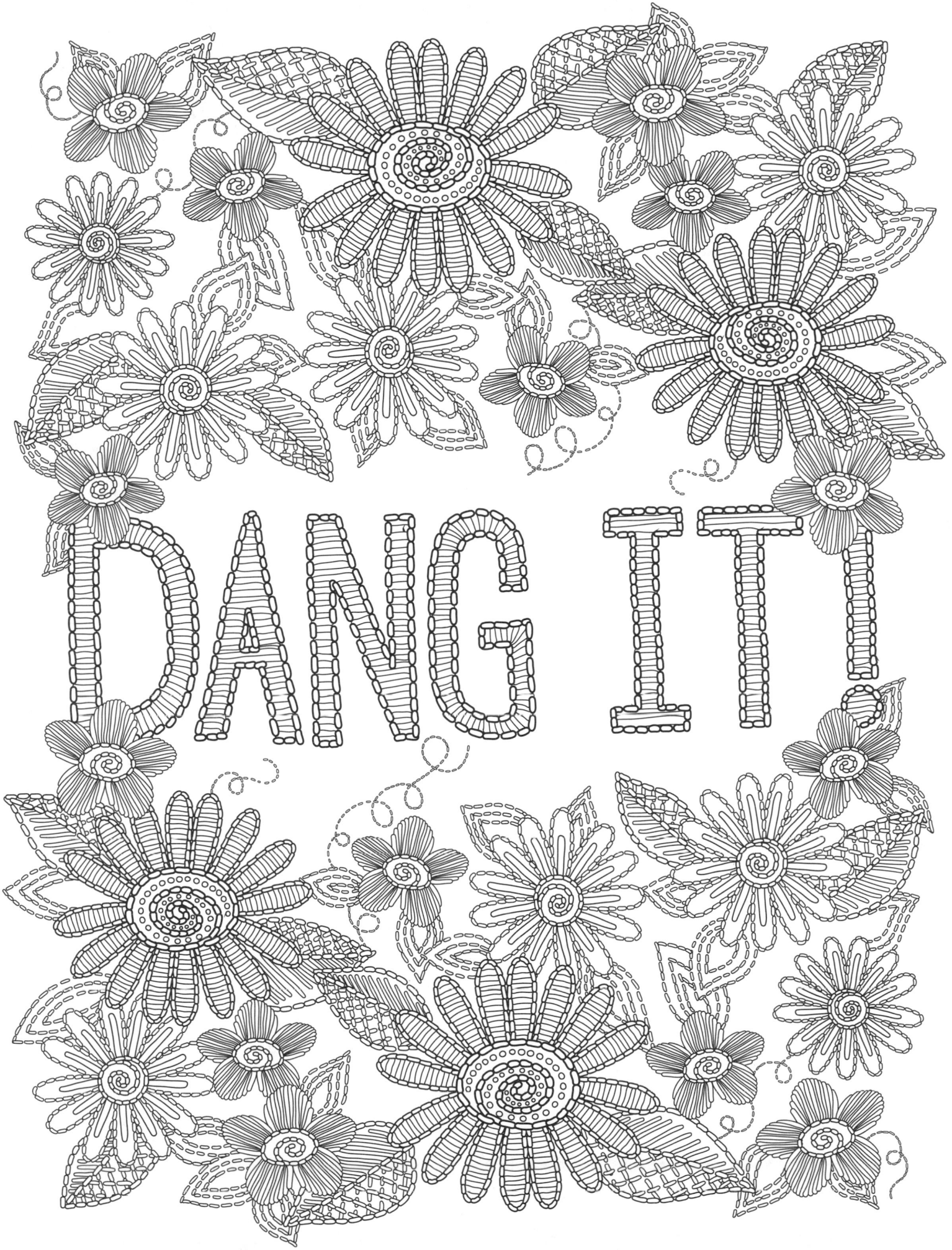
DANG IT

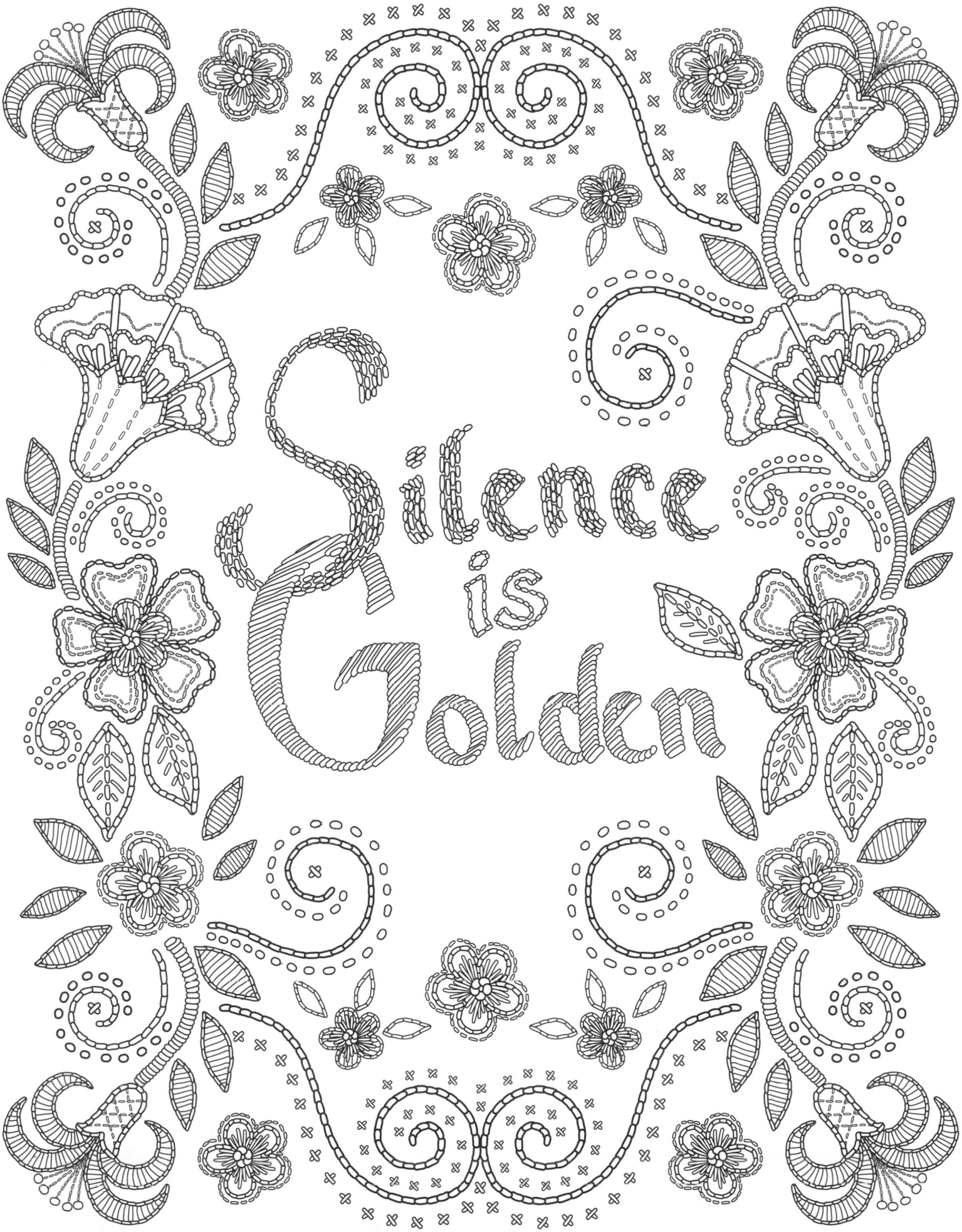
Silence
is
Golden

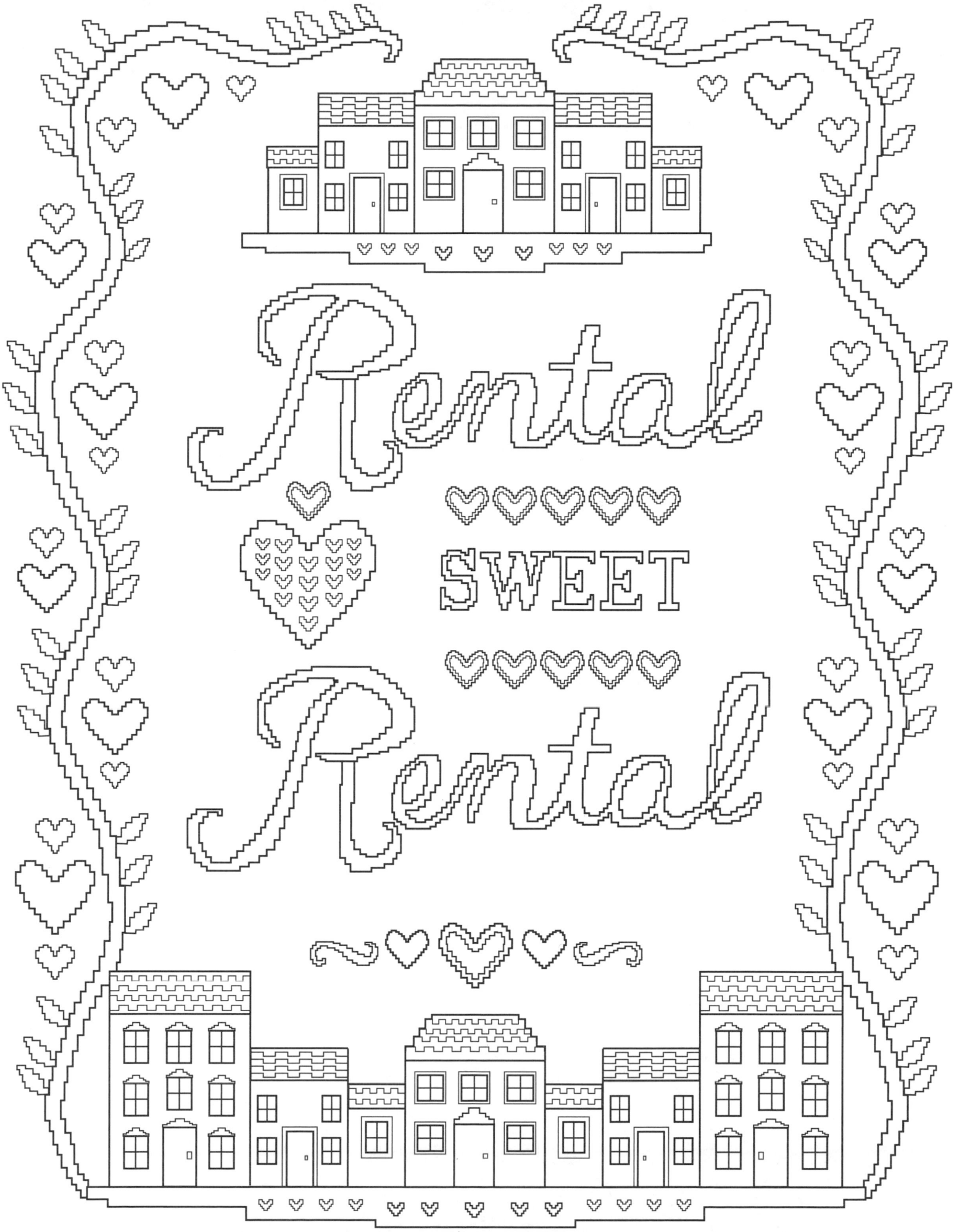
Rental
SWEET
Rental

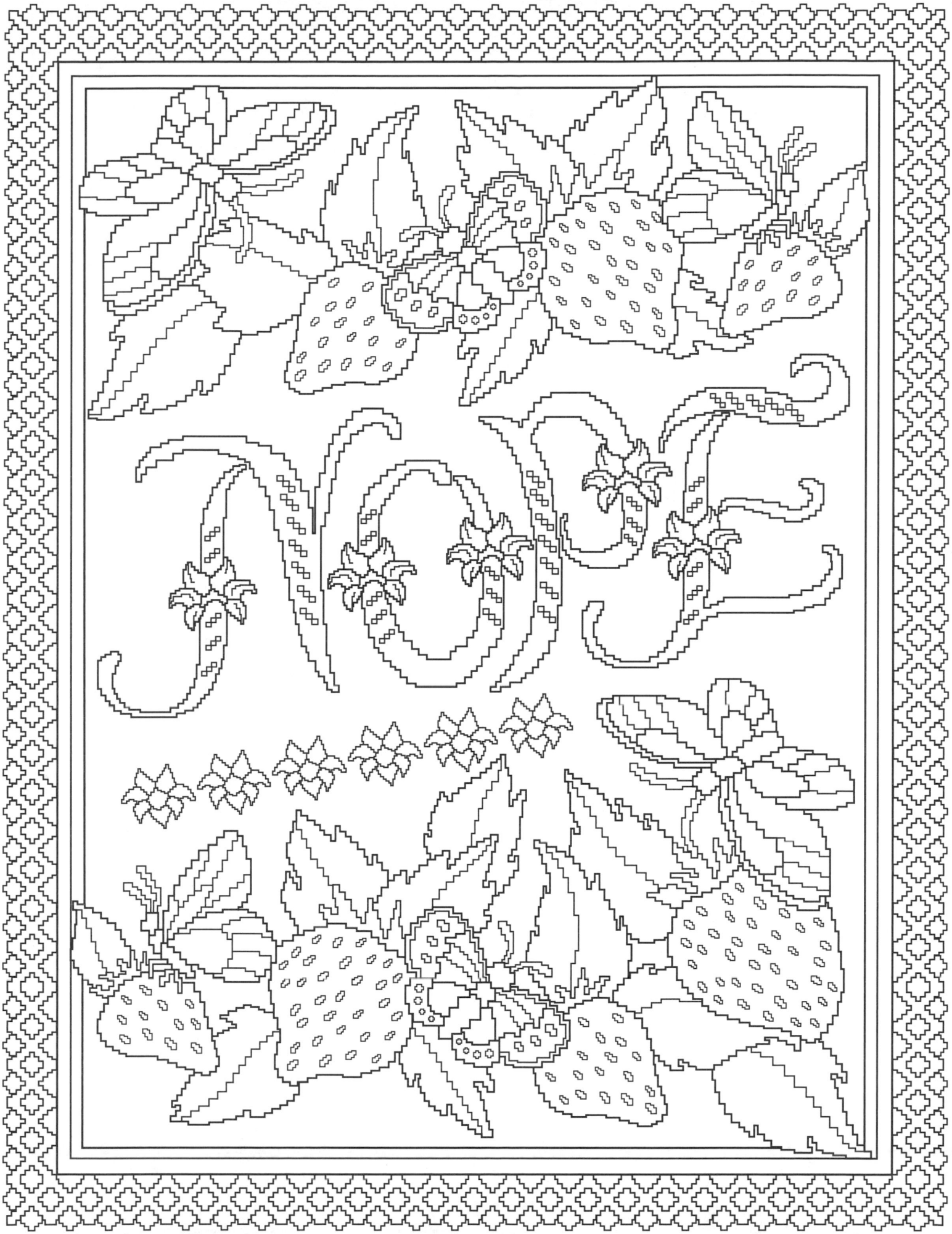
ROSE

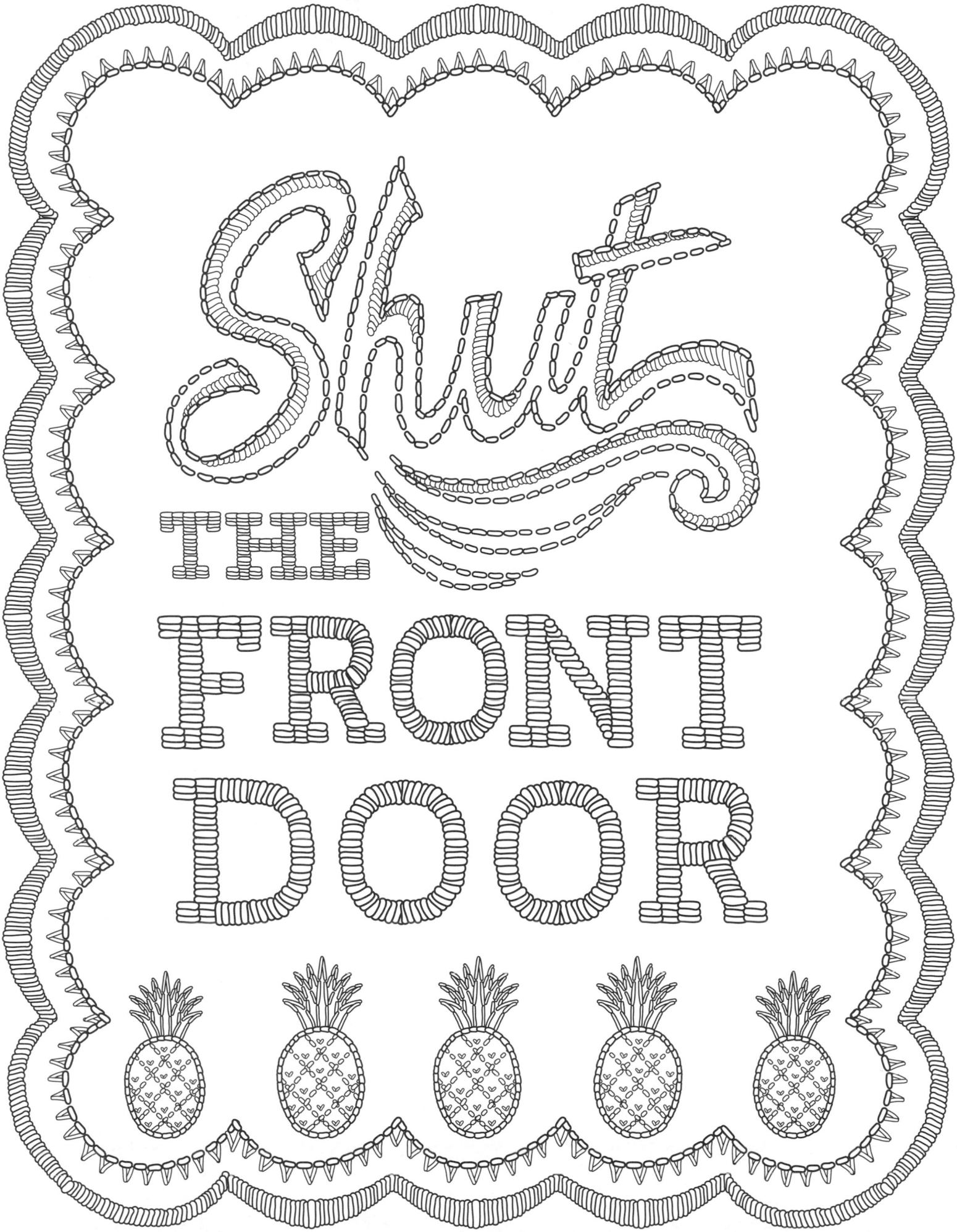
Shut
THE
FRONT
DOOR

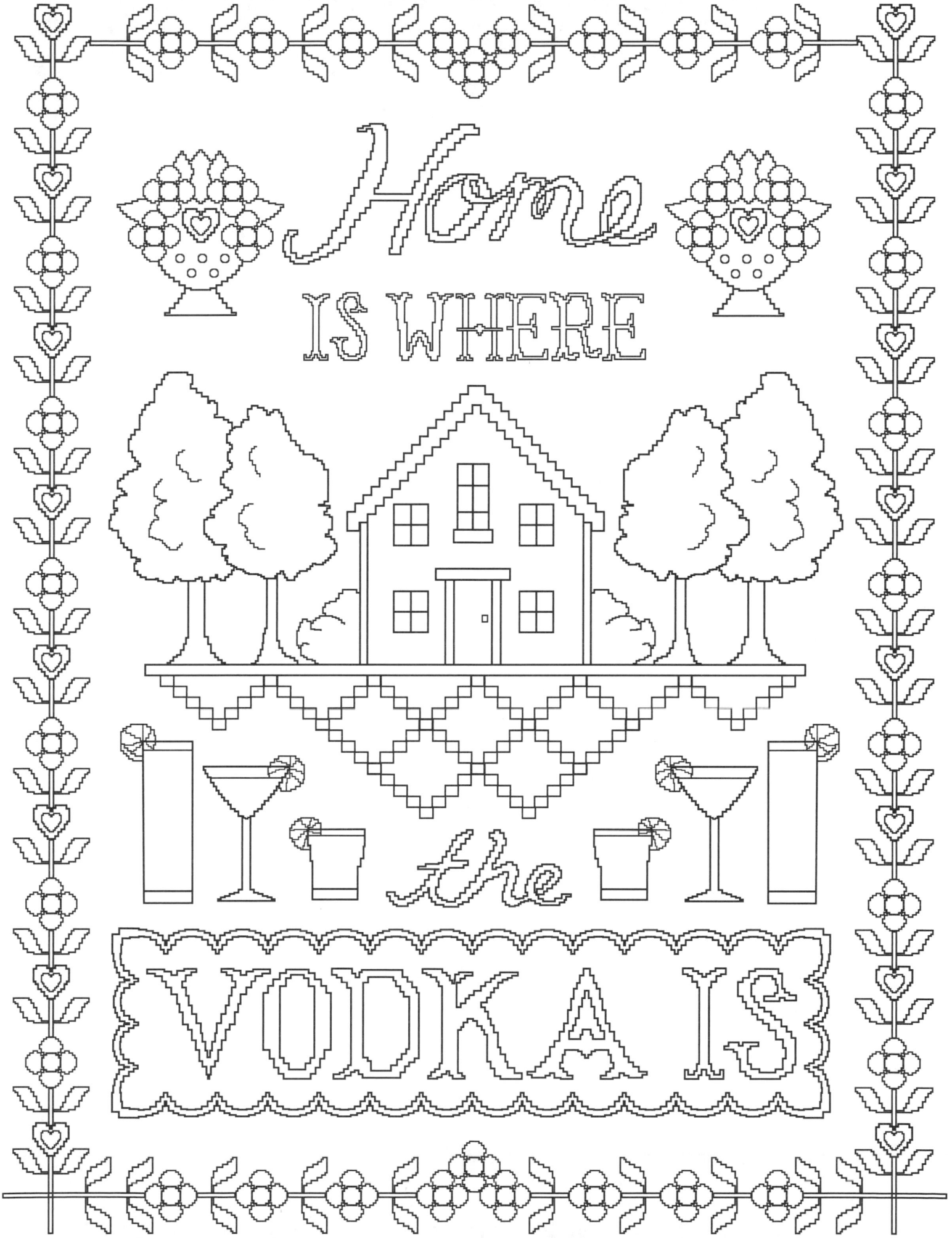
Home
IS WHERE
the
VODKA IS

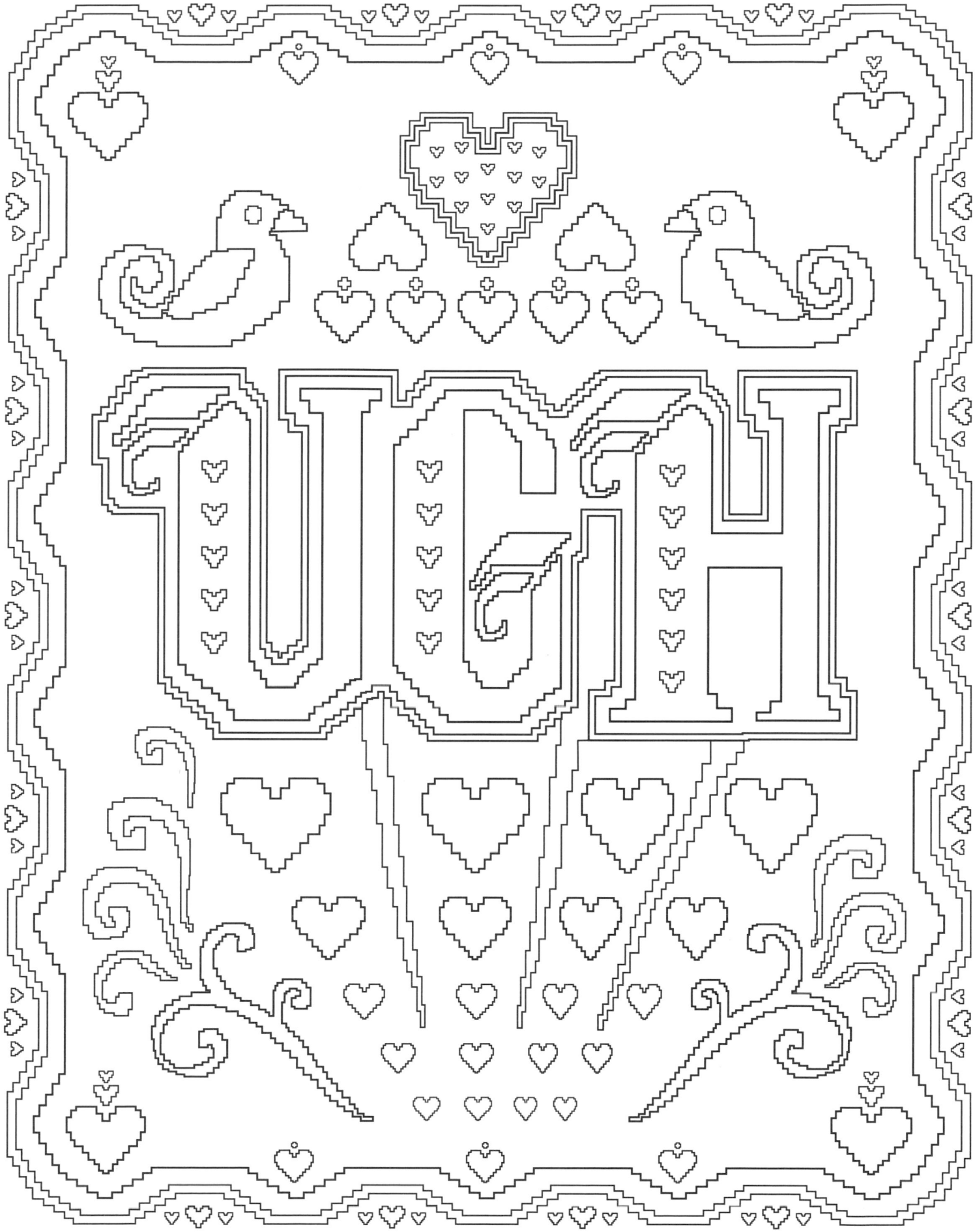
HUGS

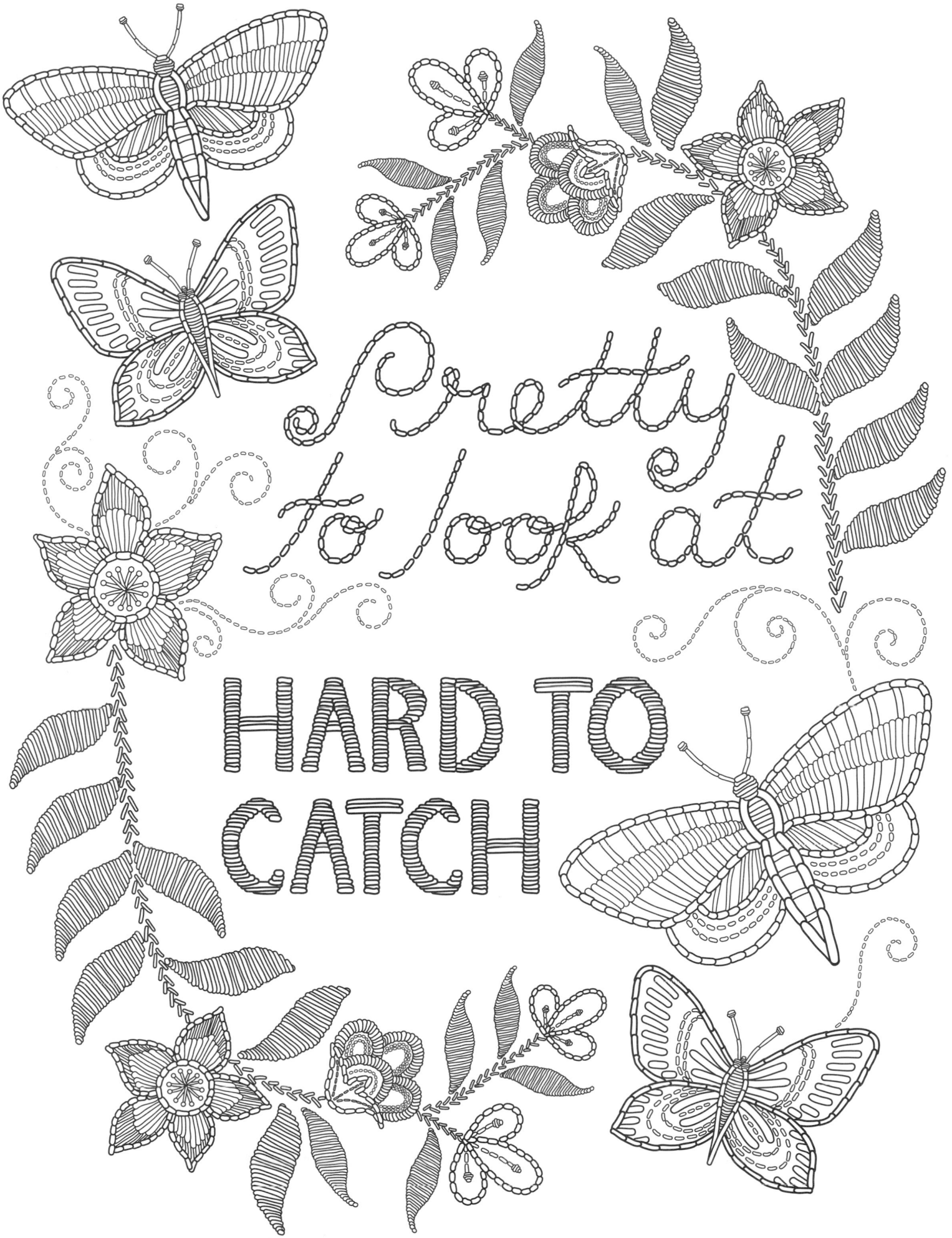
Pretty
to look at
HARD TO
CATCH

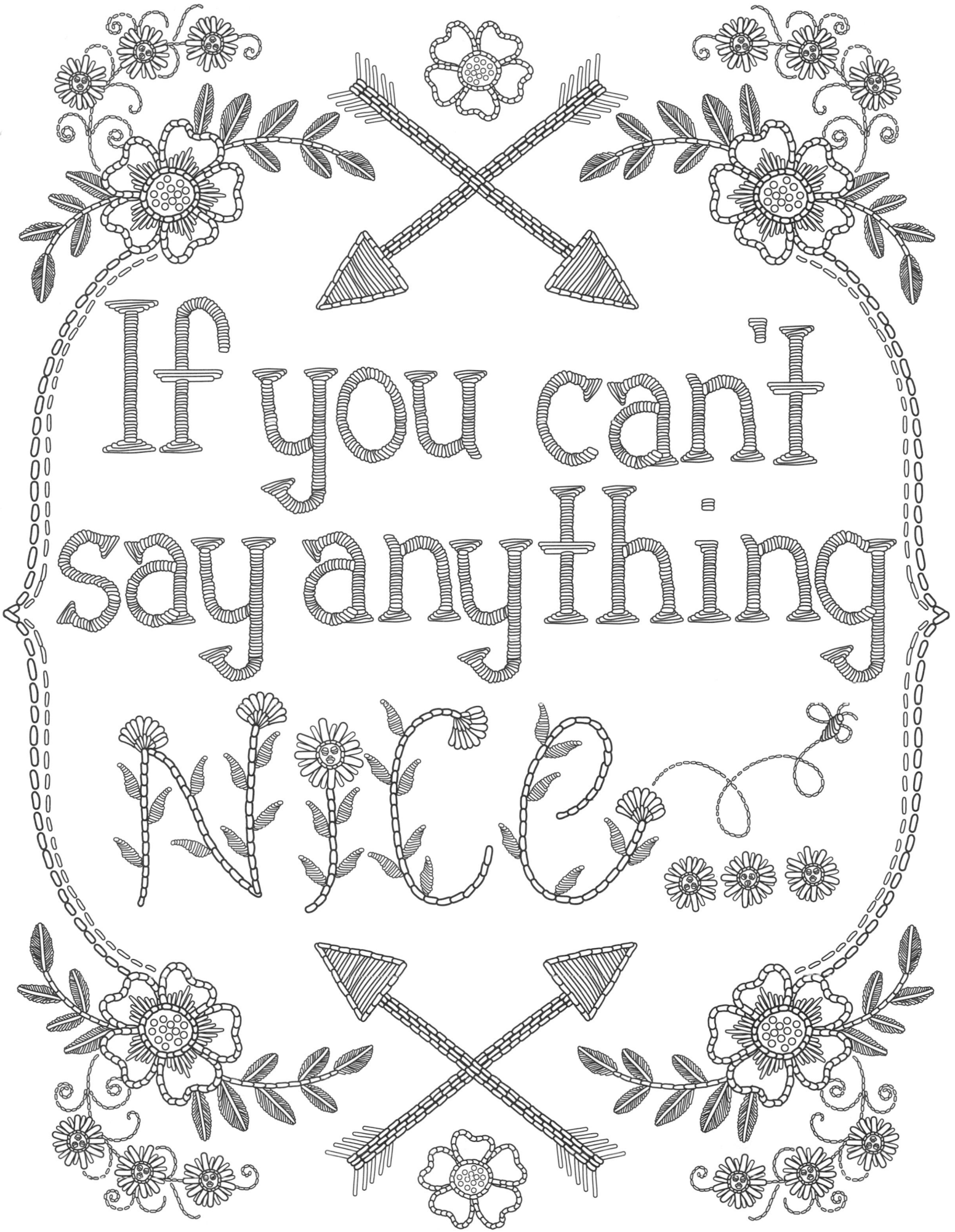
If you can't
say anything
NICE

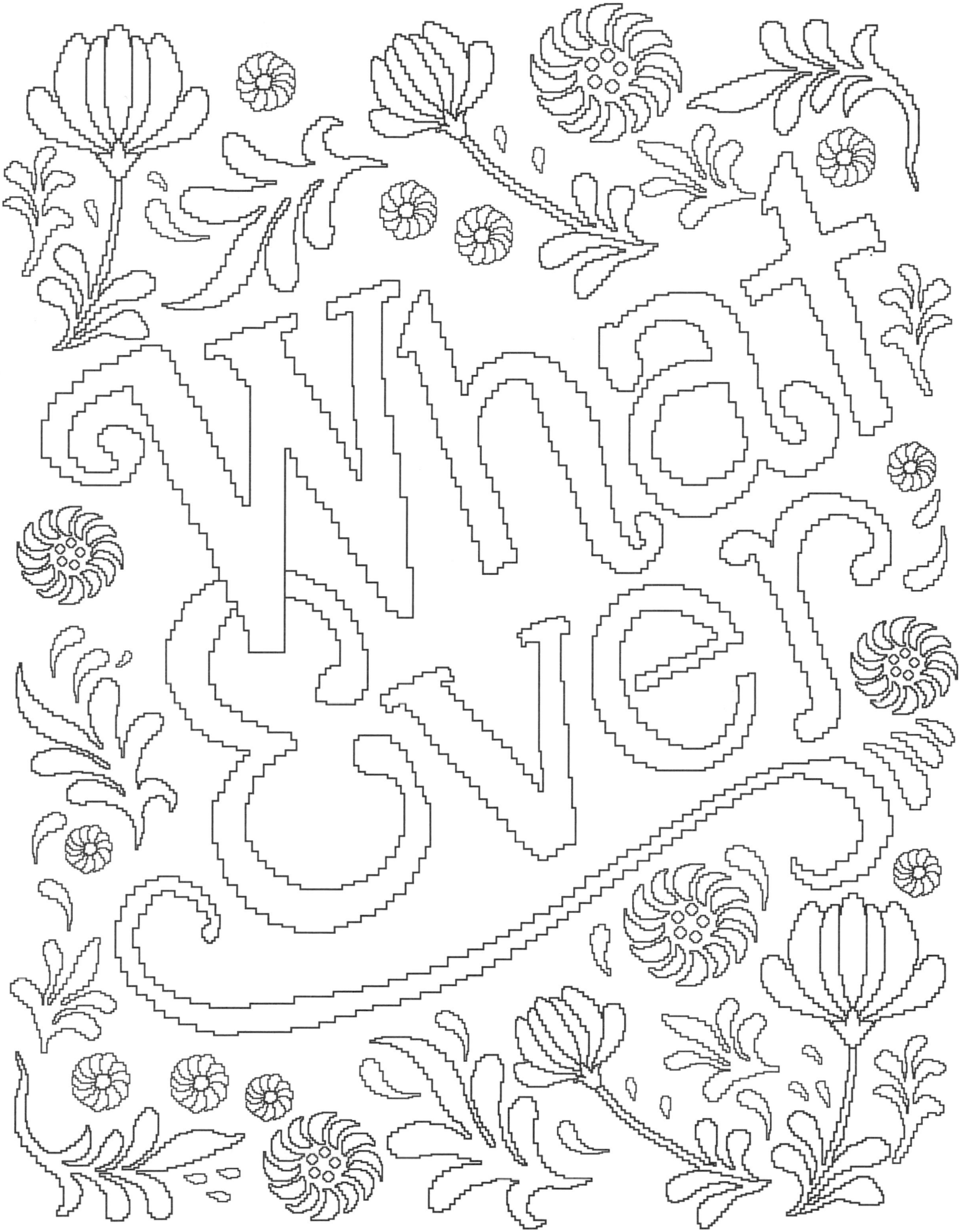
Almost
Done

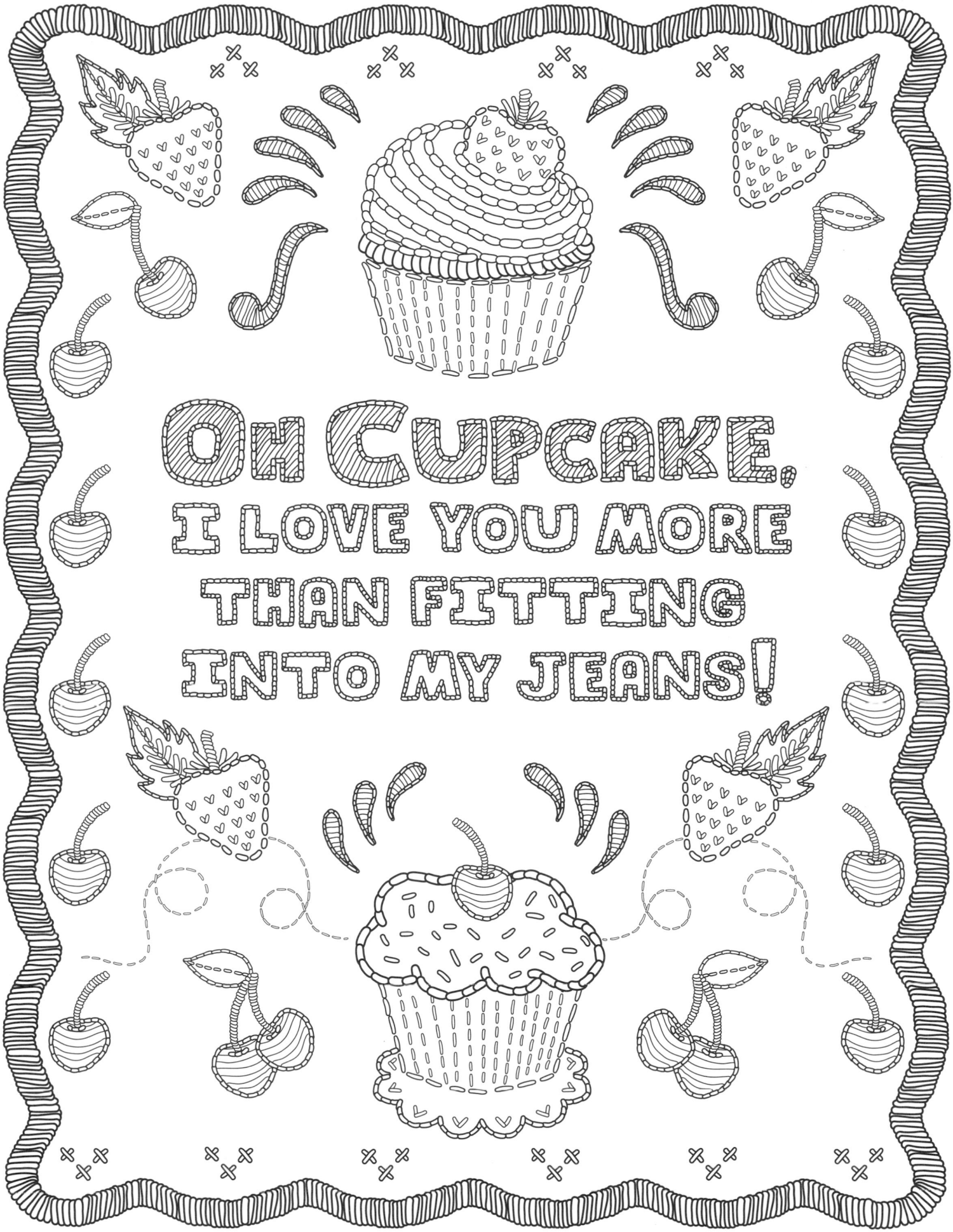
OH CUPCAKE,
I LOVE YOU MORE
THAN FITTING
INTO MY JEANS!

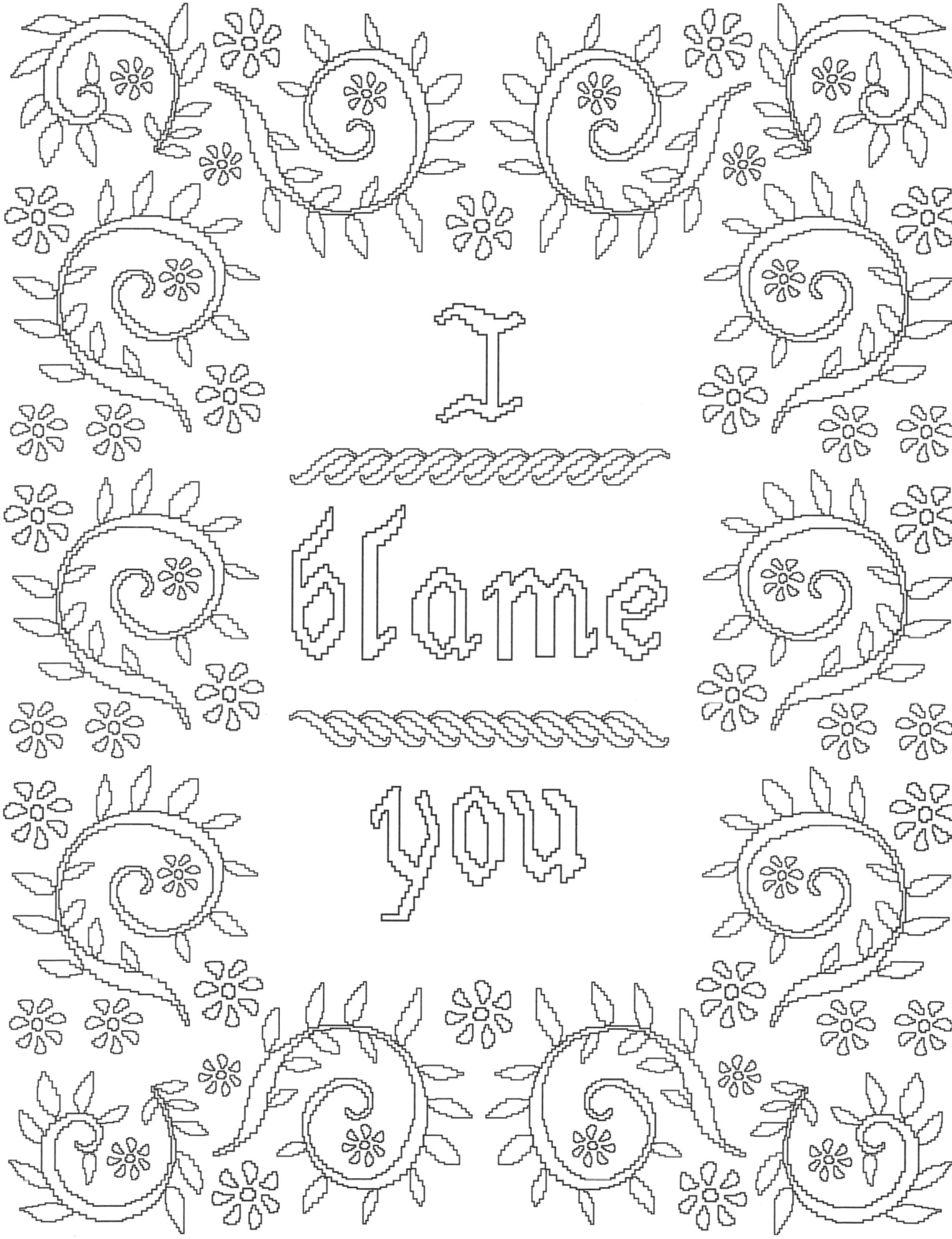
I
blame
you

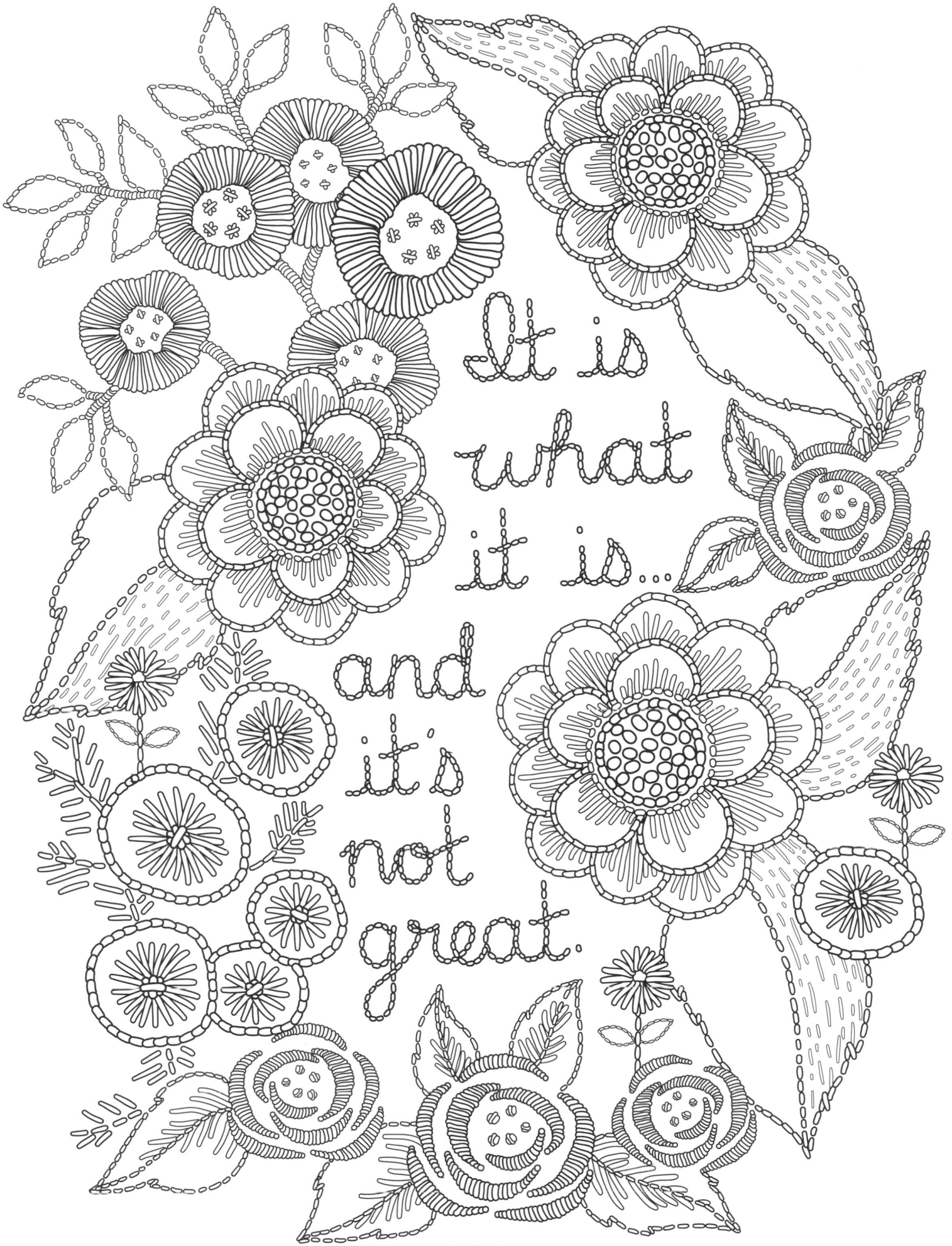
It is
what
it is...
and
it's
not
great.

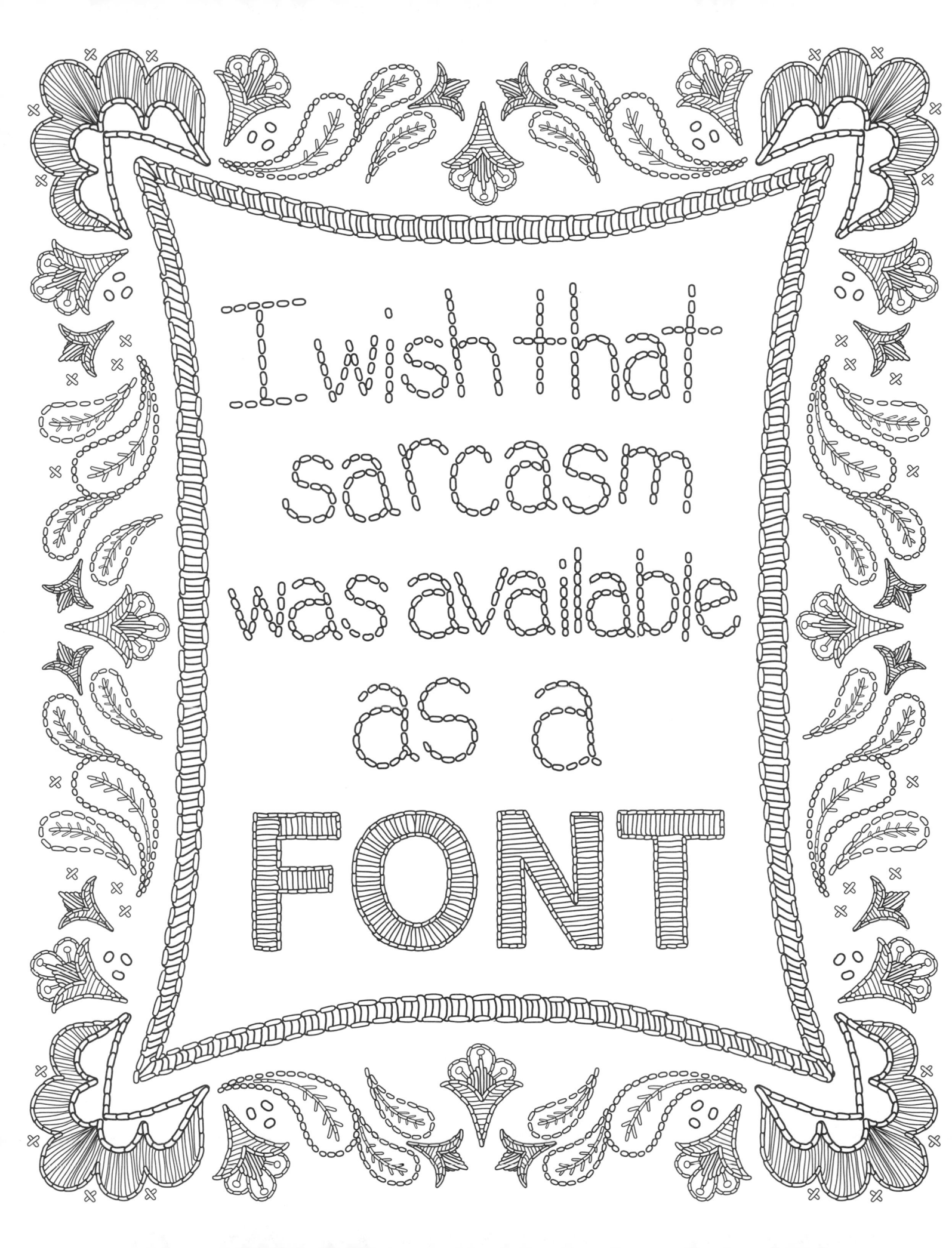
I wish that
sarcasm
was avalabe
as a
FONT

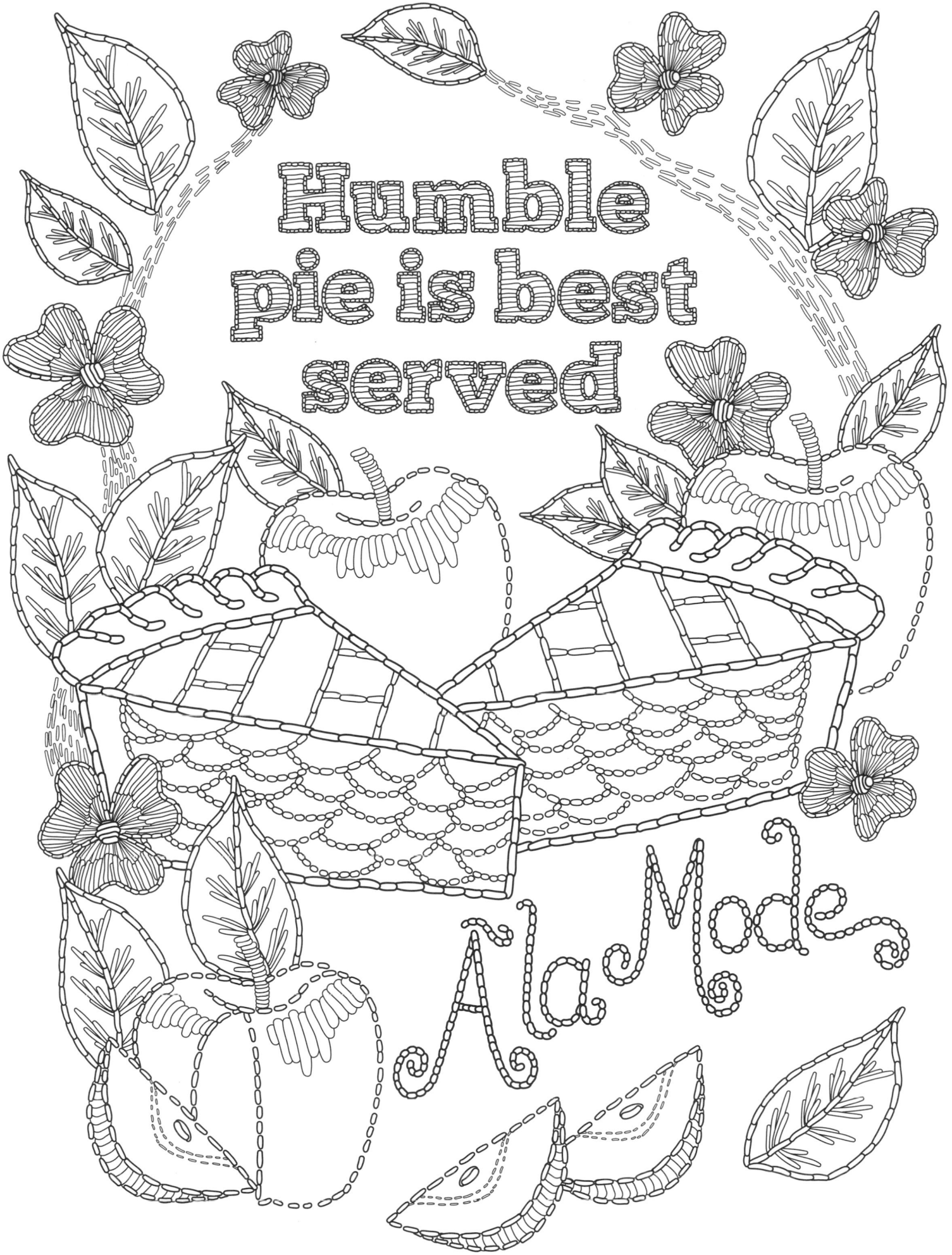
Humble
pie is best
served
Ala Mode

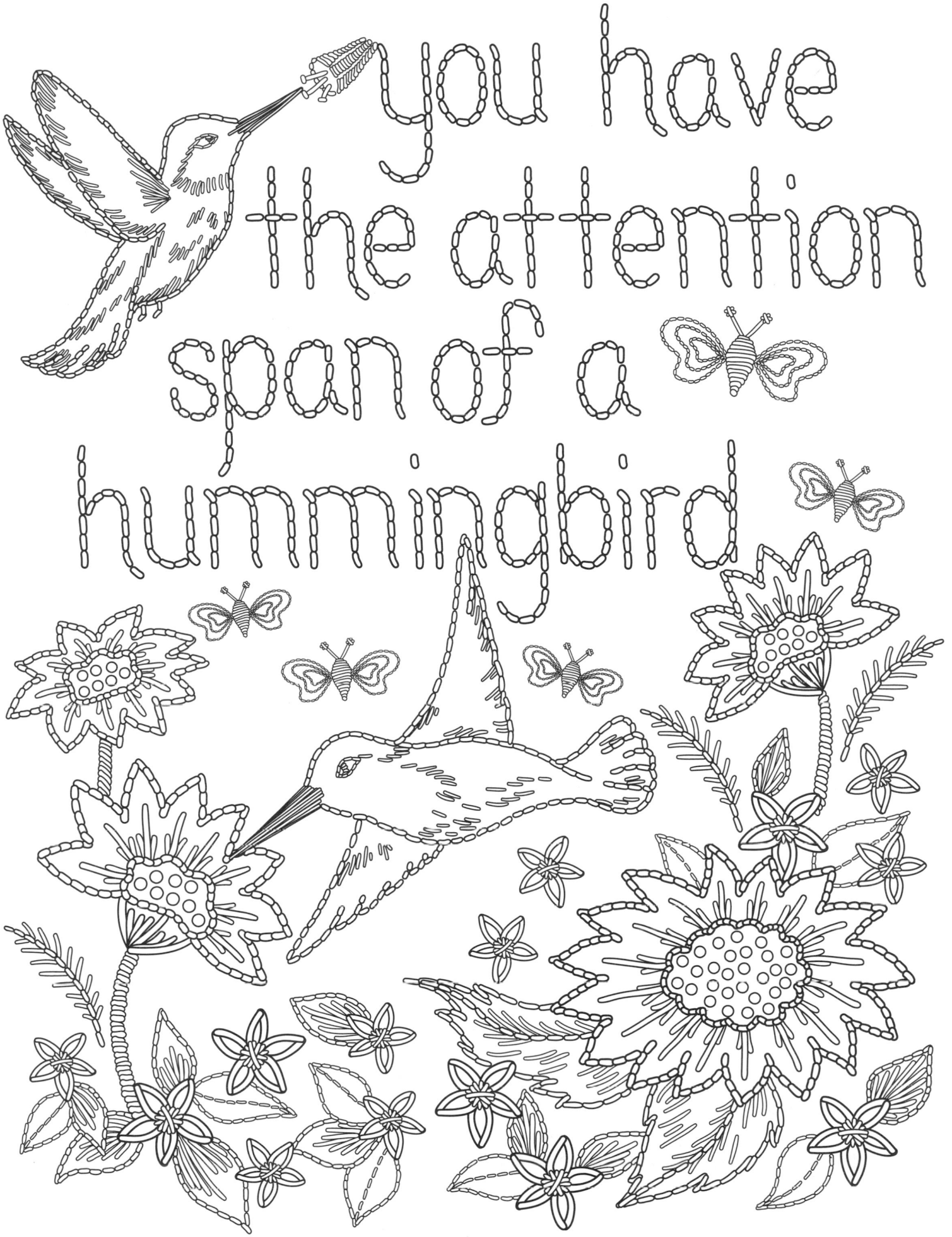
you have
the attention
span of a
hummingbird

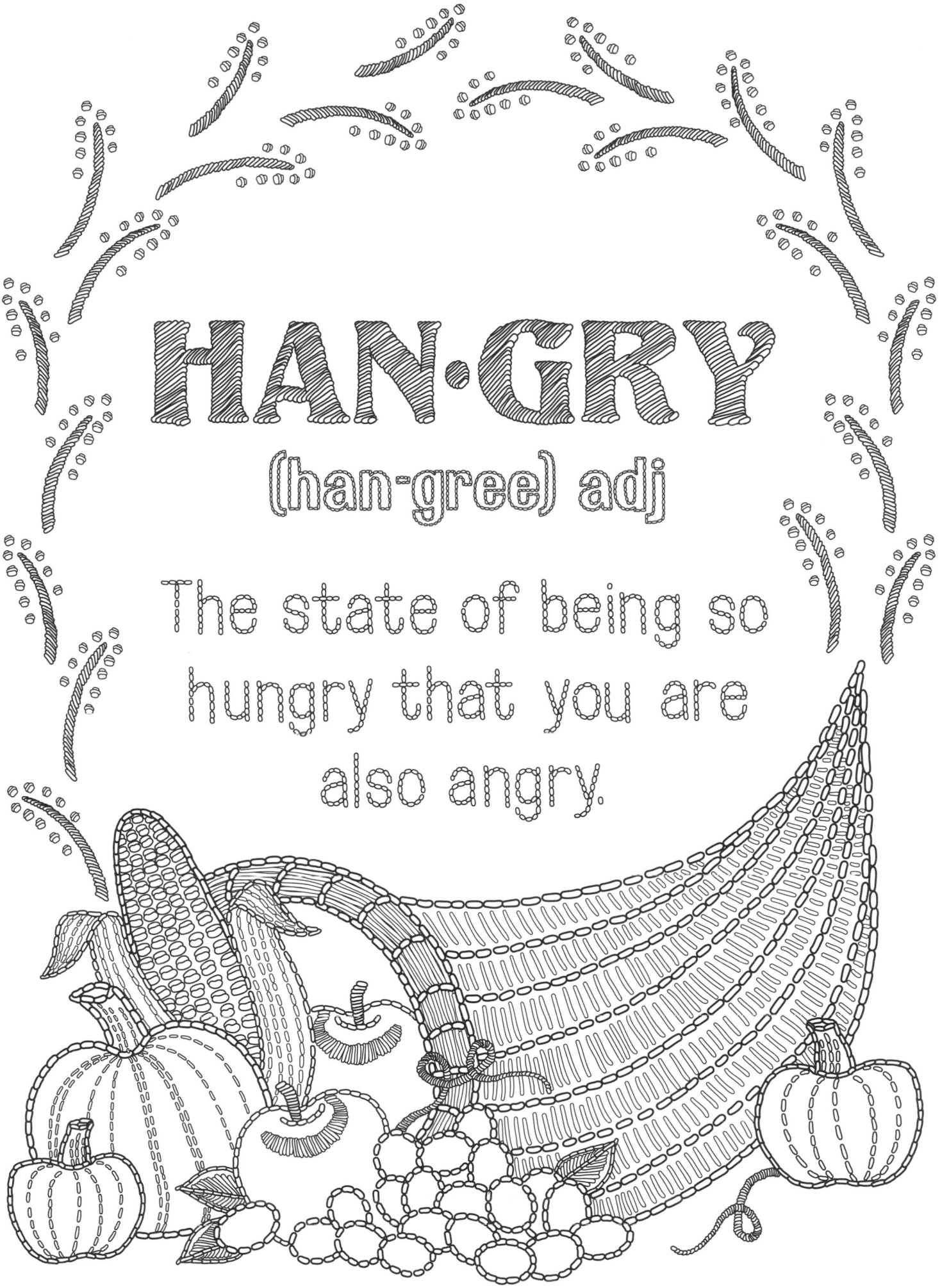
HAN·GRY
(han-gree) adj
The state of being so hungry that you are also angry.

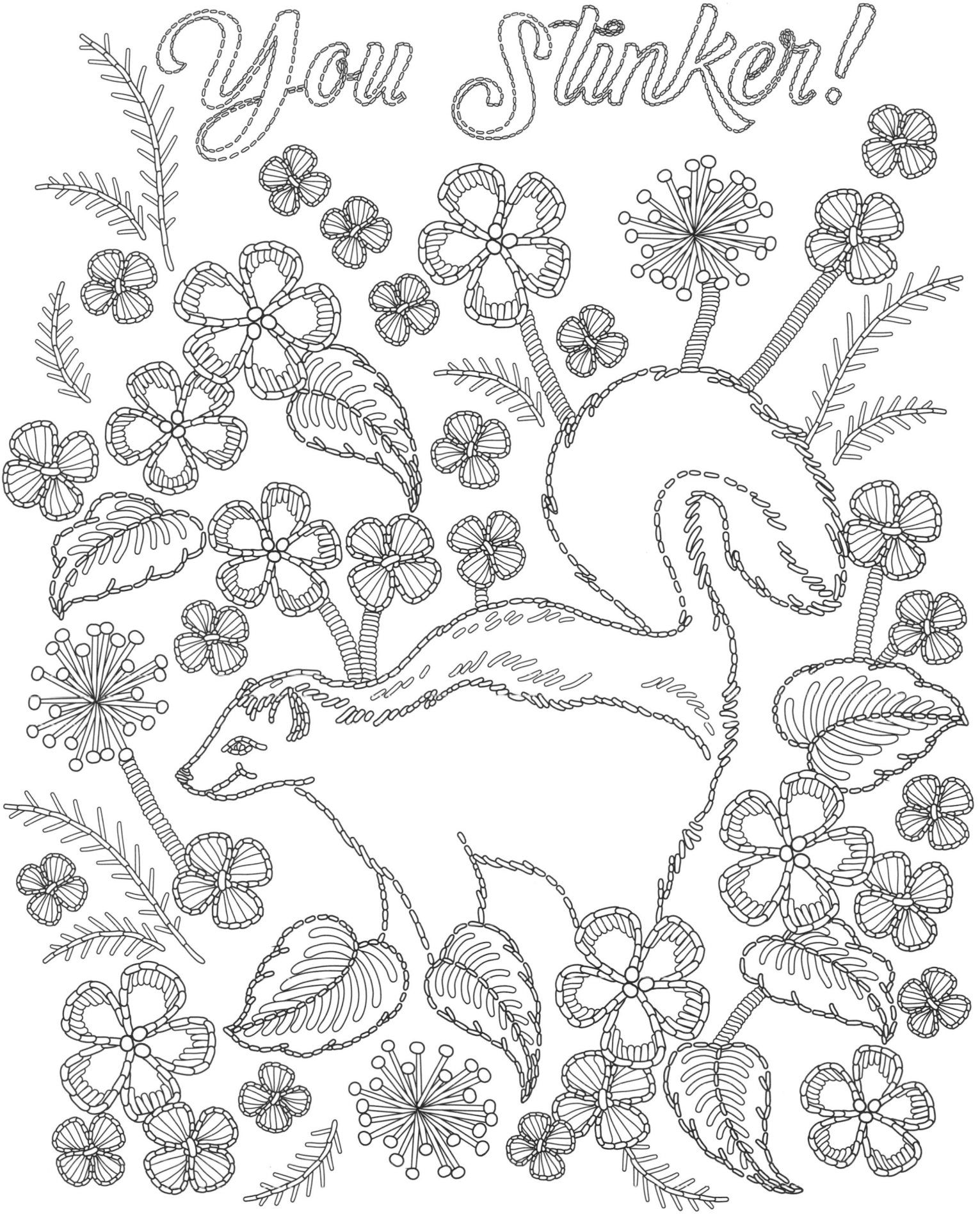
You Stinker!

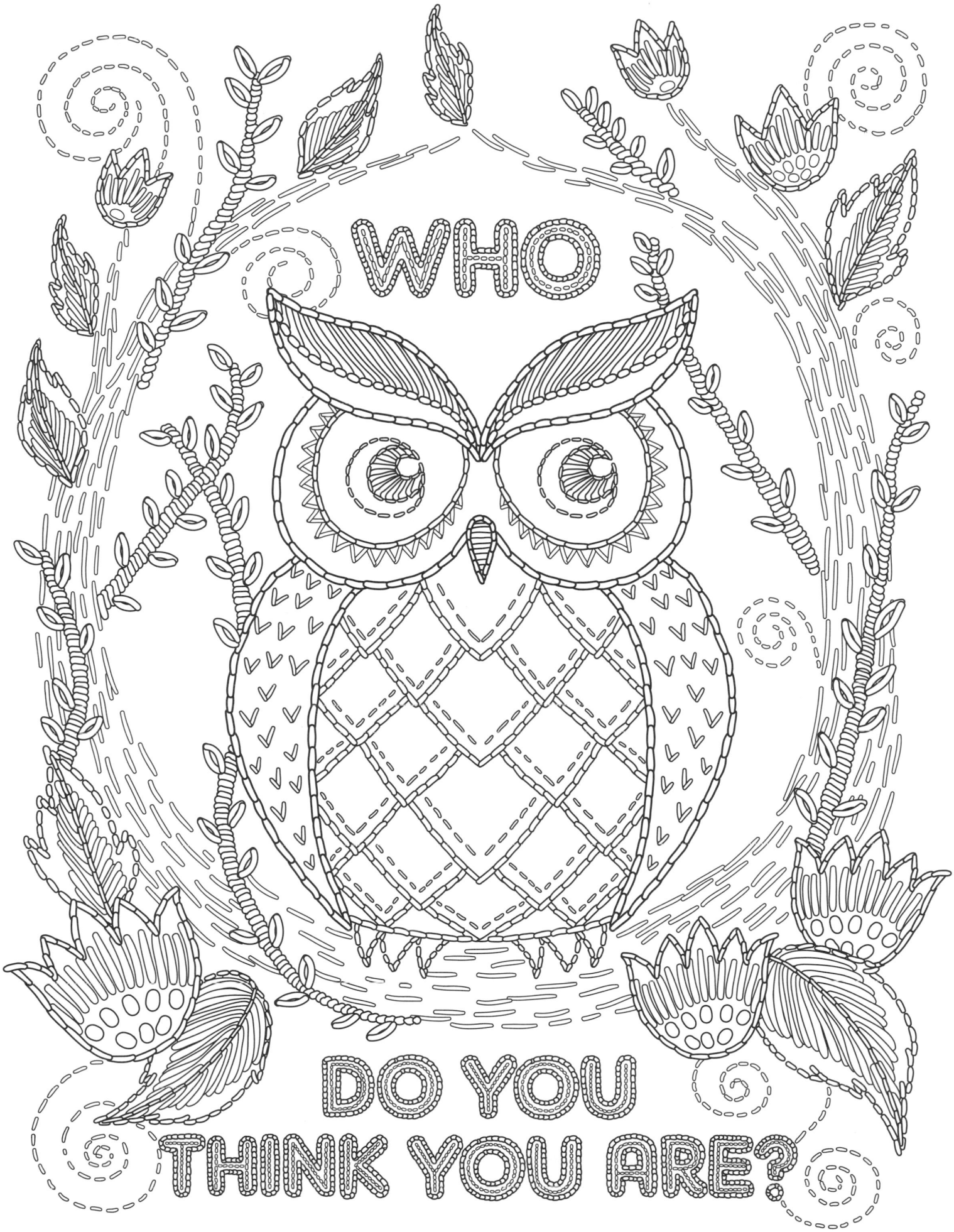
WHO
DO YOU
THINK YOU ARE?

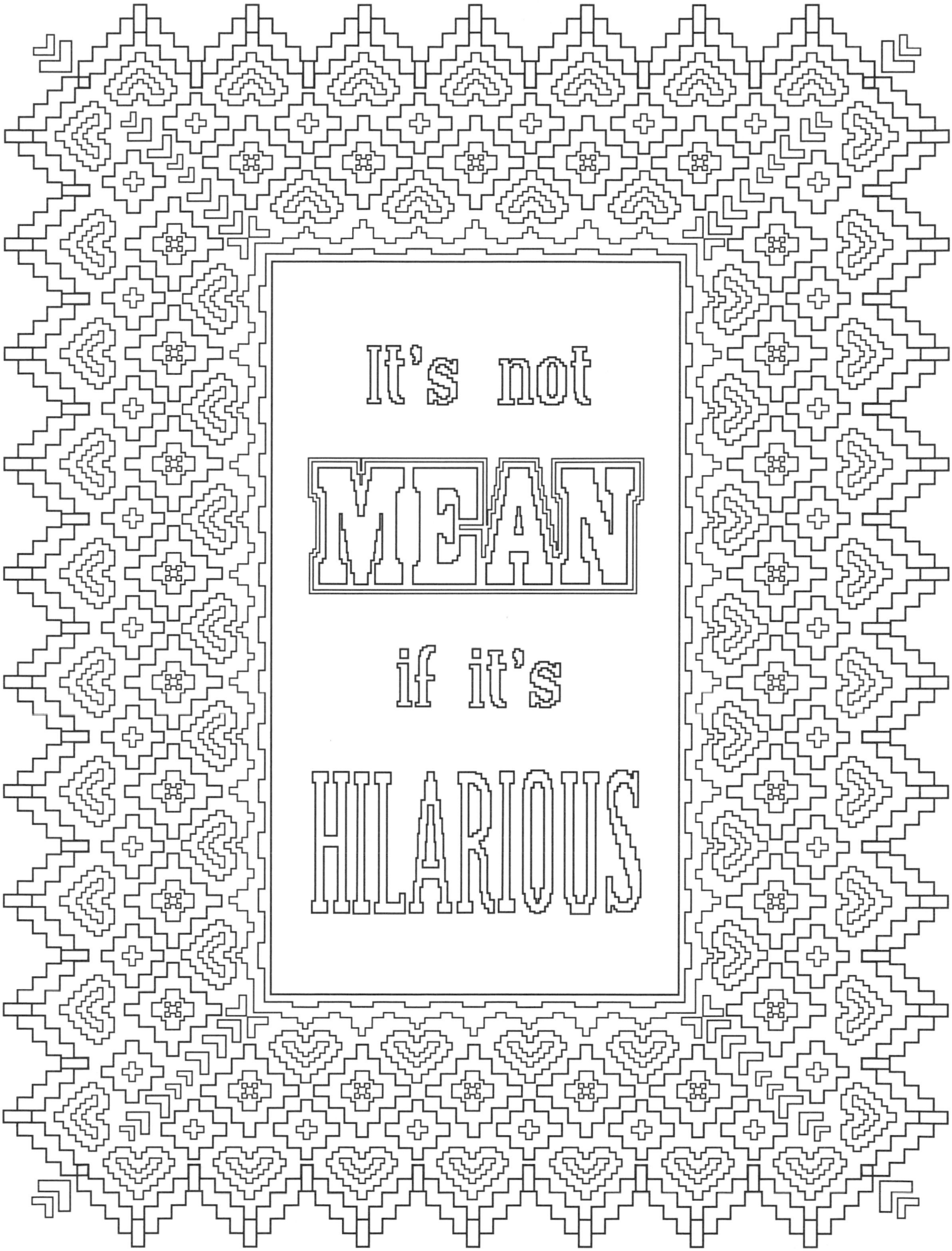
It's not
MEAN
if it's
HILARIOUS

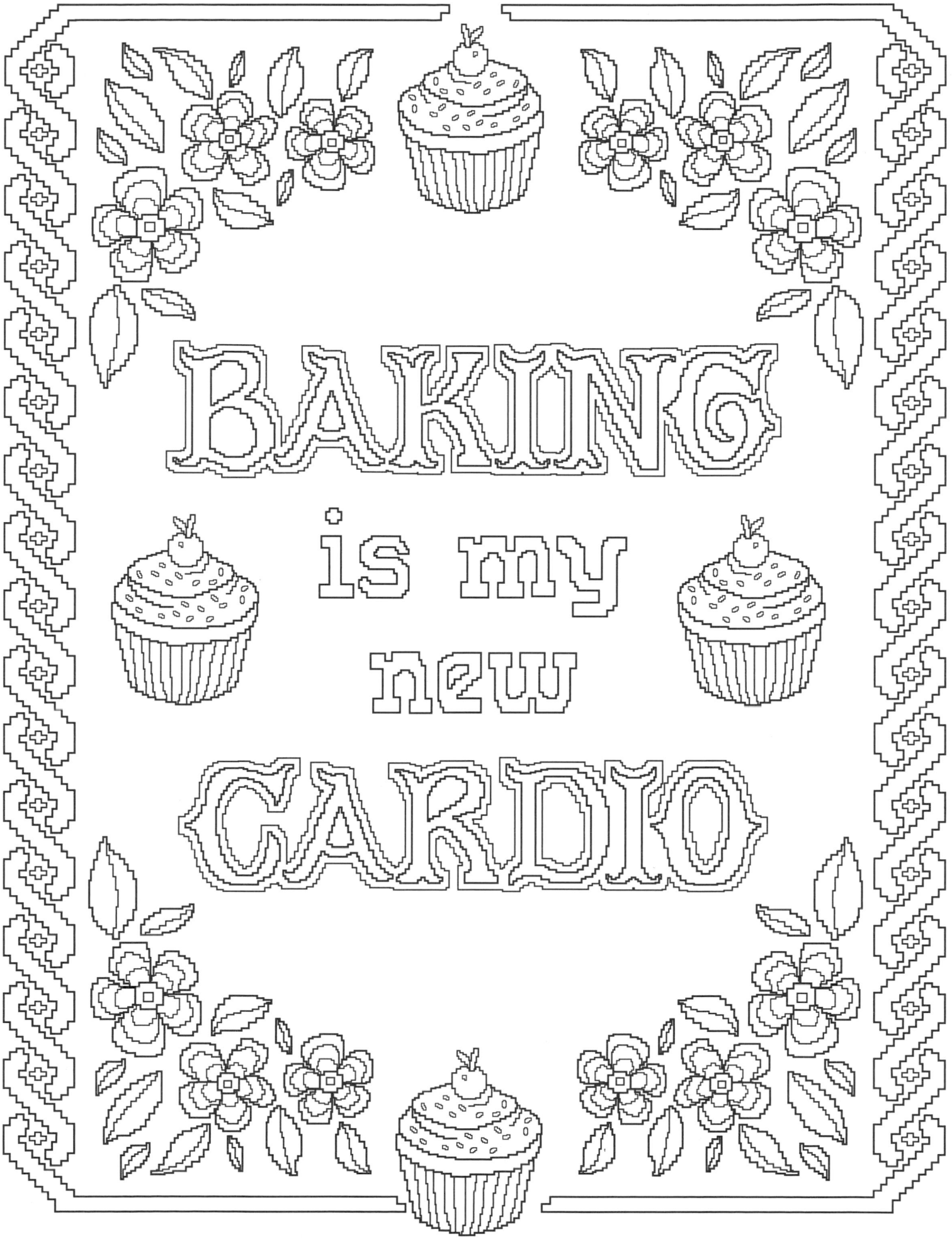
BAKING
is my
new
CARDIO

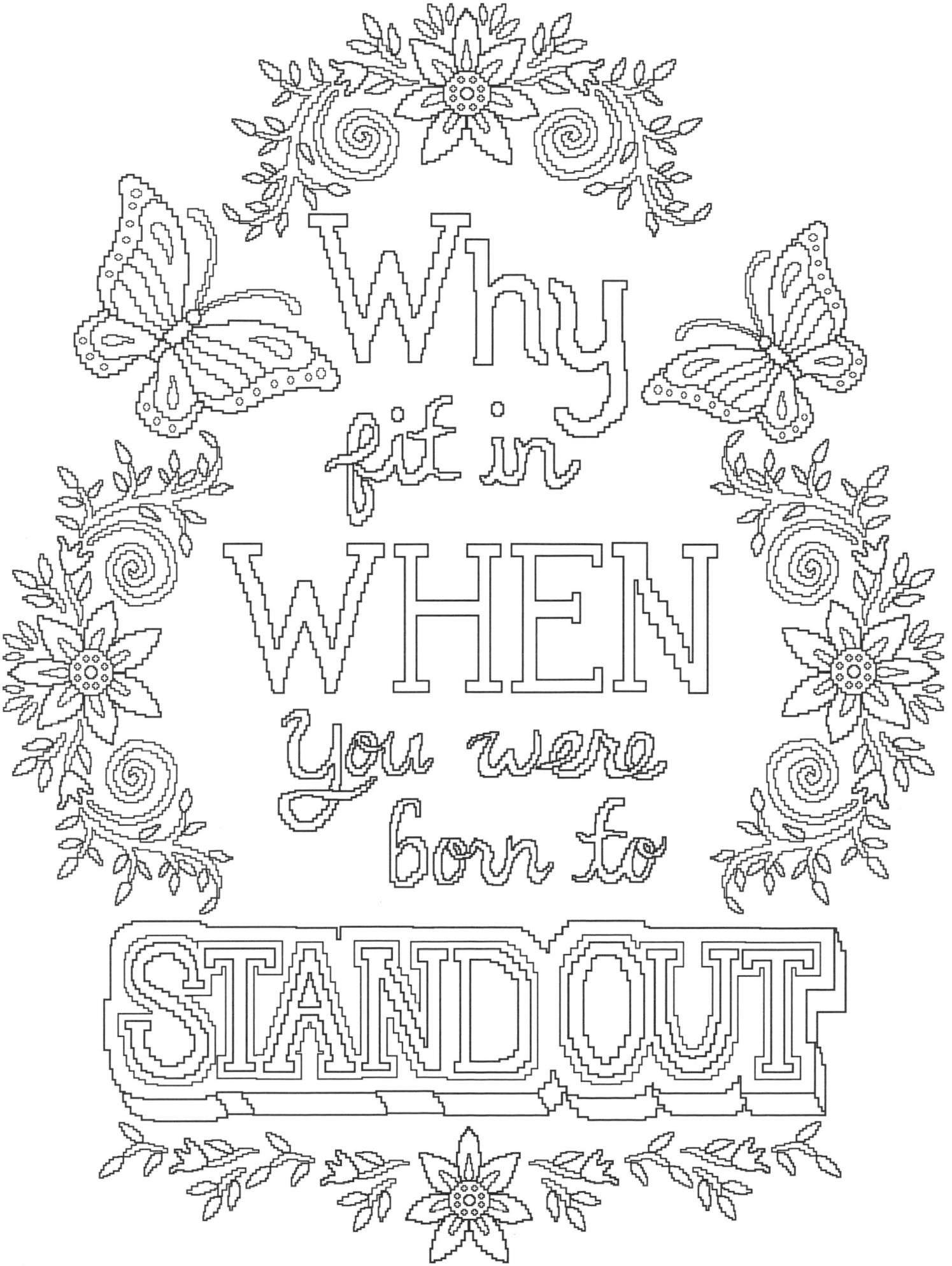
Why fit in
WHEN
You were born to
STAND OUT